middle school survival guide for anxious kids

Calm-Down Tools, Confidence Builders, Friendship Scripts, Study Routines, and Social Media Tips To Go From Awkward to Awesome in Just 30 Days

Growing Up Chronicles

introduction

It's the first day of sixth grade. You're standing in the hallway with your brand-new schedule in one hand and your phone (which you're not even sure you're allowed to have out) in the other. You've just realized that Room 214 is definitely not near your locker, and you have exactly four minutes to get there. Oh, and your locker? The one with the combination you've practiced opening seventeen times at home. Yeah, it's jammed. Meanwhile, a group of eighth graders breezes past you like they own the place (spoiler: they kind of do), and you're pretty sure you just saw your crush disappear around the corner. Cool. Totally not awkward at all.

If this sounds even a little bit familiar - or if just reading it made your stomach do that weird flip thing - you're in the right place. Middle school is a wild ride. It's exciting and terrifying, full of new freedoms and confusing rules, amazing friendships and unexpected drama. One minute you're laughing with your friends, and the next you're wondering why nobody laughed at your joke in English class. You're figuring out who you are, what you like, and how to navigate a world that suddenly feels way more complicated than elementary school ever was.

Here's the thing: I'm not going to stand here and pretend I have all the answers, or that middle school is going to be perfect if you just follow some magic formula. That's not real life, and you deserve better than that kind of fake positivity. What I can tell you is that I've been there - I've survived the awkward moments, the friendship drama, the tests I wasn't ready for, and yes, even the jammed lockers. And I've talked to lots of middle schoolers who are living it right now.

They've shared their biggest fears, their most embarrassing moments, their best survival hacks, and the things they wish someone had told them on day one. That's why I wrote this book. Because middle school shouldn't feel like you're stumbling through a maze blindfolded, hoping you don't crash into a wall. You deserve something that actually gets what you are going through - someone who understands that you're worried about way more than just homework and a hall pass. You're worried about where to sit at lunch. Whether that text you sent sounded weird. If everyone can tell you're nervous during your presentation. How to handle it when your best friend suddenly seems closer to someone else. What to do when you see something mean about you in a group chat. So here's what makes this guide different from all those other "how to survive middle school" books written by adults who graduated in, like, 1987: This book is packed with real stories from actual middle schoolers, not made-up scenarios that feel fake. You'll find scripts for those moments when you freeze up and can't think of what to say.

Checklists for staying organized when your brain feels like a browser with 47 tabs open. Strategies for handling stress, anxiety, and big emotions that don't involve sitting in a field of daisies meditating (though hey, if that's your thing, no judgment). And most importantly, you'll find advice that reflects the world you're actually living in - complete with group chats, social media, and all the complicated stuff that comes with being a middle schooler in 2026.

Inside these pages, you'll discover how to:

- Navigate your first day (and first week, and first month) without losing your cool or your locker combination
- Build real friendships - and know when to walk away from toxic ones
- Handle gossip, rumors, and drama without becoming part of the problem
- Stand up to bullying (whether it happens in the hallway or online) and support others who need it
- Manage stress, anxiety, and mood swings that can make you feel like you're on an emotional rollercoaster
- Stay organized with homework, tests, and about seventeen different things due on the same day
- Communicate with teachers, parents, and peers - even when it feels scary or awkward
- Navigate group chats, social media, and digital life without drama, oversharing, or regret
- Build genuine confidence (not fake "just be yourself!" nonsense) and bounce back from embarrassing moments
- Take care of your body and brain with habits that actually fit into your busy, chaotic life

- Set goals you actually care about - and learn from the inevitable fails along the way

And here's the best part: You don't have to read this book in order. Seriously. If you're freaking out about a group project tomorrow, flip straight to the chapter on communication. If you're feeling invisible in the cafeteria, jump to the friendship section. This isn't a textbook - it's your secret weapon. Use it however you need it, whenever you need it. Dog-ear the pages, highlight the good stuff, write in the margins. Make it yours.

Throughout this book, you'll also find something we call the "Glow Up Tracker." No, this isn't about makeup or fashion (though if that's your thing, cool). Your "glow up" is about growth - real, messy, awkward, awesome growth. It's about noticing when you do something brave, even if it doesn't go perfectly. It's about celebrating the small wins, like finally remembering your locker combo on the first try or speaking up in class even though your heart was pounding. The Glow Up Tracker is your space to record these moments, reflect on what you're learning, and see just how far you've come. Because here's a secret:

You're already glowing up, even if it doesn't always feel like it. Middle school is messy. It's uncomfortable. You will have days when you feel like everyone has it figured out except you. You'll say things you wish you could take back, forget things you swore you'd remember, and have moments that make you want to crawl under your desk and hide until high school. But you know what else? You'll laugh until your stomach hurts. You'll discover things about yourself you never knew. You'll make friends who get you. You'll have adventures (even if some of those adventures are just surviving Tuesday). And you'll come out the other side stronger, braver, and way more capable than you ever thought possible.

So, take a deep breath. Grab your backpack (and maybe a snack - I'm a big believer in snacks). And let's do this. Middle school doesn't stand a chance.

You've got this.

welcome to middle school - decoding the vibe

Surviving Day One Without Losing Your Chill

The Vibe Check: What Day One Really Feels Like

It's 7:23 AM. You're standing in front of your mirror wearing the third outfit you've tried on this morning. Your stomach feels like you swallowed a butterfly convention. Your phone keeps buzzing with texts from friends asking, "Are you nervous?" (which, honestly, is not helping). And you're pretty sure you've checked your backpack four times already, but... maybe you should check it again? If this is you right now, or if it was you a few weeks ago, let me tell you something important: You are so not alone.

Real Middle Schoolers on Day One:

> "The night before sixth grade, I couldn't sleep. I kept having this nightmare that I showed up in my pajamas, and everyone was pointing and laughing. Spoiler: I did NOT show up in my pajamas, but I was so tired from not sleeping that I almost walked into the wrong building."
>
> — Maya, 7th grade

> "I thought I was going to throw up on the bus. Like, actually throw up. I texted my mom, and she said, 'That's just nerves, you'll be fine.' She was right, but I definitely didn't believe her at the time."
>
> — Jordan, 6th grade

"Honestly? I was kind of excited. But also terrified.
It's like being excited and terrified at the exact same
time, which is a really weird feeling."

— Aisha, 8th grade

See? Everyone feels some version of this. The butterflies, the outfit changes, the random panic about forgetting something important - it's all completely normal. Your brain is basically doing its job: paying attention when something new and potentially important is happening. So, if you're nervous? That just means your brain is working. Good job, brain.

Your First Morning Game Plan

Okay, so you can't control everything about your first day (like whether your locker will cooperate, or if the cafeteria will have something edible), but you CAN control how you start the day. Here's your step - by - step morning routine:

1. Eat Something (Yes, Really)

I know you might not feel hungry. Your stomach is probably doing Olympic gymnastics. But trust me on this: having anything in your stomach will help. You don't need a five-course breakfast - just grab a granola bar, some toast with peanut butter, a banana, or whatever. Just don't go in empty. Your brain needs fuel, especially when it's working overtime to remember locker combinations and avoid walking into poles.

Quick wins: Granola bar + water bottle, yogurt + fruit, English muffin with cream cheese, or, honestly, leftover pizza if that's what gets food in your body.

2. Pick Your Outfit the Night Before (But Have a Backup Plan)

Here's the truth about first - day outfits: You're going to see people wearing everything from designer brands to their favorite ratty hoodie, and literally nobody will remember what you wore by lunchtime. The goal isn't to impress everyone - it's to wear something that makes YOU feel comfortable and confident.

The vibe you're going for: *"This is me, I'm comfortable, and I'm ready for whatever."* Think about what you'd wear on a good day when you're hanging out with friends - not trying too hard but not looking like you rolled out of bed either.

Pro tip: Have a backup outfit ready. If you wake up and that first choice suddenly feels wrong (this happens to literally everyone), you've got plan B waiting. No morning meltdown required.

3. The Triple - Check Backpack System

- Pack your backpack the night before, then do the morning check. Here's what you actually need on day one:
- Your schedule (screenshot it on your phone too - backup is key)
- A notebook or folder (even if they haven't given you supply lists yet)
- Pens and pencils (at least three - someone will ask to borrow one)
- Your lunch or lunch money
- Phone (charged!) if your school allows it
- A water bottle (those hallways get warm, and you'll be walking a lot)
- Any forms your school sent home (signed by a parent if needed)
- Emergency snack (trust me on this)

What you DON'T need on day one: All your binders, every supply list item, your entire locker decor collection. They'll probably spend day one handing out info and going over rules anyway. You can bring the rest later.

Awkward Moment Survival Guide: Do's and Don'ts

Something awkward is probably going to happen. You might walk into the wrong classroom. You might trip in the hallway. You might forget someone's name three seconds after they tell you. This is not a disaster - it's just... Tuesday. Here's how to handle it:

Scenario: You Walk Into the Wrong Classroom

🚫**DON'T:** Freeze in the doorway like a deer in headlights or try to slowly back out while everyone stares.

✓ **DO:** Give a quick *"Oops, wrong room!"* with a smile and leave like it's no big deal (because it isn't). Bonus points if you can make a joke: *"Not my math class? My bad!"* Then check your schedule and move on.

Or try, *"Sorry, wrong room!"* or *"Is this room 214? No? My bad!"* Short, friendly, done.

Scenario: You Trip in the Hallway

🚫**DON'T:** Pretend it didn't happen (everyone saw), or freak out like it's the end of the world.

✓ **DO:** Laugh it off. Seriously. Make a joke at your own expense: *"That floor came out of nowhere!"* or *"I'm fine, my ego hurts more than my knee!"* People will laugh WITH you, not AT you.

These could also work: *"I'm good! Just practicing my gymnastics!"* or *"Well, that was graceful."* Then keep walking. By tomorrow, literally no one will remember.

Scenario: You Forget Someone's Name Immediately

🚫**DON'T:** Avoid them for the rest of middle school or call them *"Hey, you."*

✓ **DO:** Just be honest. Everyone forgets names, especially when you're meeting seventeen new people in one day. Just say, *"Hey, I'm so sorry - I met like ten new people this morning, and my brain is fried. Can you remind me of your name?"*

They'll tell you, and you'll both move on.

The Ultimate "Glow Up" Guide—What Really Changes in Middle School?

Your First Day Glow Up Tracker

At the end of day one, take five minutes to fill this out. It'll help you see that even if the day felt overwhelming, you actually crushed it in ways you didn't even realize.

Three things that made me nervous today:

1.

____

2.

____

3.

____

Three wins I had today (even small ones):

1.

____

2.

____

3.

____

Examples of "wins": *Found all my classes without getting lost, said hi to someone new, survived lunch without a major disaster, opened my locker on the first try, made someone laugh, asked a teacher a question, texted a friend about something funny that happened.*

ONE THING I'm proud of myself for:

____

____

OKAY, so you've survived day one. But you're probably wondering: What's actually different about middle school? Like, really different - not just "it's in a bigger building" different. Let's break it down.

Elementary School vs. Middle School: The Real Talk

Here's a comparison chart that shows what's actually different (and what's basically the same, just with more drama):

What	Elementary School	Middle School
Your Teachers	One main teacher (maybe two)	6-8 different teachers with different rules and personalities
Your Classes	Stay in one room most of the day	Switch rooms every 45-60 minutes (hello, hallway traffic)
Recess	Playground time built into the day	No official recess (but you get lunch and passing periods)
Your Locker	Cubby or desk for your stuff	Actual locker with a combination you have to remember
Homework	Usually from one teacher	From multiple teachers (sometimes all due the same day)
Lunch	Assigned seats or close supervision	You choose where to sit (which can be stressful)
Sports & Clubs	Mostly during school or very casual	Tryouts, practices, real commitment
Freedom	Pretty structured and supervised	More independence (but also more responsibility)
Schedule	Pretty much the same every day	Might have A days and B days, rotating schedules
Grades	Matter, but not as much	Count toward your permanent record (dramatic, but true)

WHAT SURPRISED REAL Middle Schoolers Most:

"I was shocked by how much walking you do. Like, my legs were actually sore after the first week from going up and down stairs and across the building all day."

— Diego, 6th grade

"The freedom was cool but also kind of scary? Like, nobody tells you where to go every second. You have to figure it out yourself."

— Emma, 7th grade

"I thought middle school would be all mean kids and drama. But honestly? Most people are just trying to figure it out like you are. It's not as scary as the movies make it seem."

— Marcus, 8th grade

"The homework thing is real. When you have six teachers, and they all think their class is the most important one, things pile up fast. You need a system."

— Priya, 7th grade

"Best surprise: The clubs and activities are actually really cool. I found my people in robotics club, and they're way more my vibe than kids in my regular classes."

— Alex, 6th grade

The Cool New Freedoms (Yes, Really)

Okay, so middle school comes with more responsibility, but it also comes with some actually awesome new freedoms. Here's what you can actually look forward to:

Electives: You get to choose some of your classes! Want to take art? Coding? Drama? You actually get a say in what you learn.

Clubs & Activities: Way more options than elementary school. Anime club, debate team, environmental club, whatever you're into - there's probably a club for it.

Your Locker = Your Space: It's small, but it's yours. Decorate it, organize it however you want. It's like having a tiny room at school.

Schedule Management: You're in charge of getting yourself to class on time. Nobody's walking you there. It feels more grown - up.

Social Freedom: You can sit with who you want at lunch, hang out with different friend groups, basically navigate your own social life.

Phone Policy: Most schools let you bring your phone to school (even if you can't use it during class and likely have to leave it in your locker). You're trusted with more tech.

Your Personal "Glow Up" Is a Journey, Not a Destination

Here's the thing about middle school: You're going to change. A lot. Not just physically (though yes, that too), but in who you are, what you like, how you see the world. This isn't something that happens overnight on the first day of sixth grade. It's a process that happens gradually, over weeks and months.

- *Your "glow up" isn't about becoming perfect or popular or having it all figured out. It's about:*
- *Learning who you really are (not who you think you should be)*
- *Getting braver at trying new things (even when you're scared)*
- *Making mistakes and bouncing back (like, a lot of bouncing back)*
- *Finding your people (the ones who get you)*
- *Speaking up for yourself and others (using your voice)*
- *Taking care of your mental and physical health (because you matter)*
- *Celebrating small wins (because they add up to big ones)*

Sample Glow Up Tracker: Here's a simple tracker you can use throughout the year (or make your own version):

1. **Week of:**
2. **One brave thing I did this week:**
3. **A new skill I learned or practiced:**
4. **Someone I helped or was kind to:**
5. **A challenge I faced and how I handled it:**
6. **Something I'm proud of (no matter how small):**
7. **My "awkward win" of the week (something that felt awkward, but I did it anyway):**

Lockers Unlocked - Zero - Stress Combos, Jams, and Decor Hacks

Let's talk about one of the most iconic (and potentially frustrating) parts of middle school: the locker. It's like a tiny metal closet that's supposed to hold all your stuff, except sometimes it refuses to open, or it opens when you don't want it to, or you forget the combination at the worst possible time. Here's everything you need to know to make your locker work for you, not against you.

The "Combo Cracker" Visual Guide

Most middle school lockers use combination locks. Here's the step-by-step for opening them without having a meltdown:

> Step 1: Start by turning right (clockwise) at least three full rotations to clear any previous combination.

> Step 2: Stop on your FIRST number. Make sure the little line on the dial is exactly on your number.

> Step 3: Turn LEFT (counter - clockwise) one full rotation, then continue to your SECOND number.

> Step 4: Turn RIGHT (clockwise) directly to your THIRD number. Don't pass it!

> Step 5: Pull the latch or lift the handle. If it doesn't open, start over from Step 1. Don't panic.

Memory trick: RIGHT to first, LEFT full turn to second, RIGHT to third. Write it down as "R - L - R" if that helps you remember!

Troubleshooting Common Locker Disasters

Problem: *"I tried my combo three times, and it still won't open!"*

Solution: Take a breath. Make sure you're doing the full rotations and landing exactly on each number - not close, but exact. The dial is picky. If it still doesn't work after three tries done slowly, find a teacher or counselor. Your combo might be written down wrong, or the lock might be stuck. This happens, and it's not your fault.

Problem: *"My locker door is jammed and won't close!"*

Solution: Check if something is sticking out and blocking it – a notebook corner, jacket sleeve, etc. If nothing's blocking it, don't force it. Report it to the office. They'll either fix it or give you a new locker. Forcing it will just make it worse.

Problem: *"Someone else opened my locker!"*

Solution: Combinations sometimes overlap by accident, or someone might have figured yours out. Report it to a teacher or the office immediately. They'll change your combo. Don't leave anything valuable in your locker in the meantime.

Problem: *"I forgot my combination!"*

Solution: The office has it on file. Just ask. They'll usually want to see your student ID or will look you up by name. No judgment – this happens to everyone at least once.

Organization Hacks That Actually Work

Your locker is small. Like, really small. You need a system. Here are some layouts that work:

The Classic: *Top shelf: Books/binders for afternoon classes. Middle hooks: Backpack, jacket, gym bag. Bottom: Books/binders for morning classes, lunch bag. Keep what you need FIRST at eye level.*

The Drawer System: *Get a small set of plastic drawers or stacking bins from a dollar store. Designate one drawer per subject. Stack them at the bottom of your locker. Hang the backpack and jacket on the hooks above.*

The Door Organizer: *Stick magnetic bins or baskets to the inside of your locker door. Use them for small stuff: pens, erasers, hair ties, lip balm, and emergency snacks. Keeps little things from getting lost at the bottom.*

Quick - Access Checklist:

Things you should be able to grab in 5 seconds or less:

- Your schedule (tape it inside the door if you keep forgetting)
- Pens and pencils (keep extras - people will borrow them)
- Lip balm/lotion (dry school air is real)
- Emergency snack (for when lunch is three periods away)
- Hair tie or small mirror (for quick checks)
- Locker Decor: Make It Yours (But Keep It Real)

Your locker can reflect your personality, but let's keep it functional and school-appropriate. Here are some low - budget, no - mess ideas:

Magnetic Photo Frames: Stick pics of friends, pets, and favorite quotes on the inside of the door.

Dry-Erase Board: Get a small magnetic one for notes-to-self, doodles, or just venting.

String Lights: Check if your school allows battery-powered string lights. Some do; some don't.

Wallpaper or Contact Paper: Cut to fit and stick to the back wall. Easy to remove at year's end.

Magnets: Collect fun ones or make your own. They add personality without taking up space.

Small Shelf: A magnetic locker shelf adds a whole extra level of storage.

What NOT to Do: Anything that violates the dress code if it's on your body probably violates it in your locker. No weapons (obviously), no inappropriate posters, nothing that could get you in trouble. Also, avoid anything sticky, messy, or that could attract bugs. And don't cover your vents - airflow matters.

Scripts for Locker Neighbors

If you have a locker next to someone (or share a locker), here are some scripts to make it less awkward:

Meeting your locker neighbor: "Hey! Looks like we're locker neighbors. I'm [your name]." If they're blocking your locker: "Hey, sorry - can I squeeze in really quick to grab my stuff?"

If you're sharing a locker: "Want to figure out a system? Like, you take the top hooks, and I take the bottom?" If your neighbor is messy: "Hey, no judgment, but some of your stuff is kind of spilling into my side. Can we reorganize a bit?"

Mastering the Maze - How to Not Get Lost

Let's be real: Middle school buildings are confusing. Multiple floors, wings that all look the same, room numbers that make no sense (why is Room 215 next to Room 301?). Getting lost is basically a rite of passage. But here's how to minimize the panic and find your way like a pro.

Step-by-Step Guide to Reading School Maps

Most schools will give you a map during orientation. Here's how to actually use it:

- **Find the legend:** Those little symbols telling you what's what (bathrooms, office, gym, etc.). Know your symbols.
- **Locate the main office:** This is your home base. If you're lost, you can always find your way back here and start over.

- **Identify your homeroom:** Mark it with a star or highlighter. This is where you'll start every day.
- **Map your first day schedule:** Use different colored highlighters for each class. Draw the path you'll take.
- **Note the shortcuts:** Some hallways connect. Some don't. Knowing shortcuts saves time (and stress).
- **Mark the bathrooms:** Trust me on this. Know where they are BEFORE you need them urgently.

"Landmark" Navigation Tips

Numbers and room names are hard to remember. Landmarks are easier:

Use what you can see: *"My math class is near the big trophy case," "English is across from the vending machines," "Science is on the floor with the blue lockers."* Physical features are easier to remember than room numbers.

Colors and patterns: Some schools have wing names *(like "A Wing" or "Science Wing").* Learn the color schemes - blue hallway for math, green for English, etc. This helps a lot.

The Practice Run Checklist

If your school does orientation or open house, DO THIS:

1. Walk from your locker to every class on your schedule
2. Time yourself - see how long it actually takes
3. Find at least two bathrooms you feel comfortable using
4. Locate the cafeteria and where you'll line up
5. Find the gym and the main entrance/exit
6. Ask questions if anything is confusing

Scripts for Asking Directions (Without Feeling Like a Baby)

Getting lost happens. Asking for help is smart, not embarrassing. Here's who to ask and what to say:

Ask older students: *"Hey, sorry to bother you - do you know where Room 214 is?"* or *"Which way to the C Wing?"*

Ask teachers: *"Excuse me, I'm new and trying to find my math class. Can you point me in the right direction?"*

Ask office staff: *"Hi, I'm a sixth grader and I'm a little lost. Can you help me find [teacher name]'s room?"*

Ask your hall monitor/aide: *"I think I'm in the wrong hallway. Where's the science wing from here?"*

Pro tip: Use your phone! Many schools have maps on their websites. Screenshot it and keep it handy. Or use a navigation app if your school has an indoor map available.

Real "I Got Lost" Stories (That Ended Fine)

> "I walked into an eighth - grade algebra class on the first day thinking it was my sixth - grade math class. The teacher just smiled and said, "One floor down." No one even laughed. I was so relieved." - Marcus, 6th grade

> "I got lost trying to find the gym for P.E. and ended up in the auditorium. By the time I found the right place, everyone was already dressed out. The coach just said, 'Happens every year. Hurry up.' That was it." - Sophia, 6th grade

> "I spent ten minutes looking for Room 132 before realizing there was no Room 132 on the first floor - it was on the THIRD floor. The room numbers weren't even in order! I asked a custodian, and he walked me there. Super nice guy." - Tyler, 7th grade

See? Everyone gets lost. Teachers expect it. Other students have been there. It's not a big deal.

Timetable Takeover - Crushing Schedule Confusion

If elementary school was like following a recipe, middle school schedules are like juggling while riding a bike. You've got different classes at different times, maybe rotating schedules, passing periods that feel too short, and somehow, you're supposed to remember it all. Let's make this less chaotic.

Breaking Down Your Schedule

Your schedule might look like a confusing grid of letters and numbers.

Here's how to decode it:

- Period numbers: 1st, 2nd, 3rd period, etc. This is the order of your classes.
- Class names: Math, ELA, Science, Social Studies, plus electives like Art or PE.
- Room numbers: Where you need to be. Write these down somewhere you won't lose.

- Teacher names: Who's teaching each class. Learn to spell them right for assignments.
- Times: When each period starts and ends. Know when you have extra time vs. when you need to rush.

The Master Schedule Cheat Sheet

Once you've decoded the basics, make yourself a cheat sheet for the first two weeks. Keep it in your phone and tape a copy inside your locker:

- **My locker number:______ Combo: ______**

- **Period 1:______** Room ______ Teacher _________________________

- **Period 2:______** Room ______ Teacher _________________________

- **Period 3:______** Room ______ Teacher _________________________

- **Period 4:______** Room ______ Teacher _________________________

- **Lunch:______** period, Room/Cafeteria _________________________

- **Period 5:______** Room ______ Teacher _________________________

- **Period 6:______** Room ______ Teacher _________________________

Surviving Rotating Schedules (A/B Days)

Some schools run an A/B block schedule — meaning you have different classes on different days. If yours does this, don't panic. It feels confusing for about two weeks and then becomes second nature. Tips:

- Check your schedule*every single morning* until it's memorized — not just the first day

- Set a phone reminder labeled "A day" or "B day," so you always know which one you're walking into

- When in doubt, ask a classmate or check the school's app or website — most post the day's schedule daily

When Your Schedule Is Wrong

Sometimes the schedule you receive has an error — a class you didn't sign up for, a missing elective, a conflict where two classes are at the same time. Here's what to do:

- Don't just ignore it and hope it fixes itself (itwon't)

- Go to the guidance office or counselor's office within the first week — this is the right place to fix schedule issues, not individual teachers

• Bring your schedule printout and explain specifically what's wrong: *"I requested Art, but I have two PE periods," or "I'm in sixth-grade math, but I was supposed to be in advanced math."*

• Be patient — the first week of school is the counselor's busiest week. If you can't get in right away, leave a note or ask to be added to the callback list

Script for the counselor's office: *"Hi, I think there might be an error on my schedule. I have [problem], but I was supposed to have [what it should be]. Can someone help me get that fixed?"*

You've Got More Than You Think

Here's the truth: Reading this chapter didn't just give you information — it gave you a head start that most of your classmates don't have. You know what the first morning actually feels like (and that the nerves are normal). You have a system for your backpack, your locker, your schedule, and your route to class. You know what to say when something awkward happens, because something awkward will happen, and that's fine.

Middle school isn't a test you either pass or fail on day one. It's more like a game where you figure out the rules as you go — and you've already read the player's guide.

One last thing before Chapter 2: Go easy on yourself this first month. You're going to forget things. You're going to go the wrong way. You're going to feel like everyone else has it more figured out than you (they don't — they're just better at pretending). That's all part of it.

Glow Up Recap:

✓ You know how to start the morning without a meltdown

✓ You have awkward-moment scripts ready to go

✓ Your locker is no longer a mystery

✓ You can read a school map and ask for directions without dying

✓ Your schedule makes sense — and you know what to do when it doesn't

The next chapter is where things get really interesting.

two
friendship fixes—making, keeping, and repairing connections

If Chapter 1 was about surviving the logistics of middle school—the hallways, the lockers, the schedules—this chapter is about something way more complicated: people. Specifically, finding your people, keeping your people, and handling it when friendships get messy (because they will).

Middle school friendships are intense. They can make your day amazing or completely ruin it. They shift and change in ways that feel confusing and sometimes unfair. But here's the good news: You can learn how to make real friends, navigate the drama, and come out with connections that actually matter. Let's figure this out together.

Making Real Friends (Even if You're New or Super Shy)

Let's start with the big question: How do you actually make friends in middle school? Not just people you say hi to in the hallway—real friends who get you, who you can text when something funny happens, who you actually want to hang out with.

The answer? It's a process. Not a one-conversation magic trick. Here's how to do it.

The "Find Your Crew" Checklist

Your future best friends are probably somewhere in your school right now. You just haven't met them yet. Here's where to look:

Clubs and Activities: This is THE best place to find your people. People who share your interests = instant conversation topics. Into art? Join the art club. Like coding? Try robotics or the computer club. Drama, chess, debate, environmental club, anime club—whatever you're into, there's probably a club for it.

Sports and Teams: Even if you're not super athletic, there are all levels of teams. You bond with teammates fast because you're working toward something together. Plus, built-in hangout time at practices and games.

Shared Classes: That kid who sits near you in science? The one who laughed at the same thing you did? That's a potential friend. Classes give you natural reasons to talk: homework questions, project partners, studying together.

Electives: Art, music, tech classes—these are where people relax and show their real personalities. It's easier to connect when everyone's creating or doing something hands-on together.

Bus/Carpool: You're stuck together every day anyway. Might as well strike up a conversation. Regular face time builds familiarity, which builds friendship.

Neighborhood/Outside School: Don't forget about kids who live near you or go to your youth group, community center, or neighborhood pool. Friendships don't have to start at school.

Action step: Join at least one thing this year. Just one. It doesn't have to be a huge commitment. Try it for a month. If it's not your vibe, try something else. But you can't find your crew if you're not putting yourself out there.

How to "Test the Waters": Building Friendship Slowly

You don't become best friends overnight. Friendship builds through small moments. Here's how to take it step by step:

Step 1: Micro-Interactions

- Start small. Really small. These don't feel like much, but they build familiarity:
- Eye contact and a smile when you see them
- A quick "hey" in the hallway
- Asking to borrow a pencil
- Complimenting something (their shoes, backpack, a project they did)
- Laughing at the same joke in class

Examples: *"Nice job on your presentation!"* or *"Cool stickers on your laptop"* or *"Did you understand what the teacher just said? I'm so confused."* Keep it casual and authentic.

Step 2: Shared Interests

Once you've established you're friendly, dig a little deeper:

- *"I saw you reading [book/manga]. Is it good?"*
- *"You play [video game]? What level are you on?"*
- *"I noticed you're into [band/artist]. Have you heard their new song?"*
- *"You're in [club], right? How is it? I've been thinking about joining."*

The goal: Find common ground. When you discover something you both like, conversations get easier and more natural.

Step 3: Mini-Commitments

This is where casual friendliness becomes actual friendship. Suggest doing something small together:

- *"Want to work on the project together after school?"*
- *"A bunch of us are going to [event/game]. Want to come?"*
- *"I'm getting lunch from [place]. Want me to grab you something?"*
- *"Want to trade numbers so we can text about homework?"*

Why this works: These are low-pressure. If it goes well, great! If not, no big deal. You're not asking them to be your best friend forever. Just... do a thing together.

Scripts for Handling Rejection (Because It Happens)

Not everyone is going to want to be your friend. That's not about you being unlikeable—it's about fit, timing, and a million other things that have nothing to do with your worth. Here's how to handle it when someone's not interested:

They say no to hanging out: *"No worries! Maybe another time."* Then move on. Don't take it personally. They might be busy, tired, or just not in a social mood.

They seem uninterested in conversation: Read the room. If they're giving one-word answers or not making eye contact, they're not into it right now. Say "Cool, see you later," and exit gracefully. Try again another day, or try someone else.

They already have a tight friend group: Some groups are just... closed. That's okay. It doesn't mean you're not worthy of friendship. It means you need to find YOUR group, not force your way into theirs.

Remember: Rejection is redirection. Every 'no' or 'not right now' is pushing you toward the people who ARE your people. Keep trying.

Journal Prompts: Tracking Your Social Victories

Friendship-building takes time, and it's easy to forget the progress you're making. Use these prompts to track your wins:

This week, I talked to:

____

One new thing I learned about someone:

____

A conversation that went well:

____

Something brave I did socially (even if it felt small):

____

Someone I want to get to know better:

____

My plan for next week:

____

Look back at this after a month. You'll be surprised by how much progress you've made.

Breaking Into a Group Without Feeling Extra or "Sus"

So you've found a group that seems cool. Maybe they're in your lunch period, or they're always together in the hallway, or they're in the same club as you. You want in. But how do you join without seeming desperate, pushy, or just... awkward?

First, let's figure out if this group is actually open to new people.

The "Group Vibe" Checklist: Are They Open or Closed?

Not all groups are welcoming to new members. Here's how to read the room:

✓ **OPEN GROUP VIBES:** Body language is relaxed and outward-facing. They make eye contact with people outside the group. They laugh and talk at a normal volume (not whispering). When someone new approaches, they shift to make room. They naturally ask questions or include others. Their conversations are about general topics, not just inside jokes.

⚠ **NEUTRAL GROUP VIBES:** They're friendly but focused on each other. They might not notice you at first. Their body language isn't hostile, just... absorbed in their conversation. This group might be open, but you'll need to make the first move. Timing matters here.

🚫 **CLOSED GROUP VIBES:** They're physically turned inward (circle with backs out). They speak quietly or whisper. They have lots of inside jokes you don't understand. When someone new approaches, they stop talking or get protective of their space. They seem annoyed by interruptions. This group isn't welcoming new people right now. Move on.

Important: If you get a closed-off vibe, it's not about you. They might have had drama with a past group member, or they might just be protective of their space. Find a different group. There are other people who will welcome you.

Non-Awkward Entry Scripts

Okay, you've found an open group. Now, how do you actually join the conversation? Use shared activities or contexts as your entry point:

In class: *"Hey, did you guys finish the homework? I'm stuck on number 5."* This gives them a reason to talk to you that feels natural.

At lunch: *"Mind if I sit here? Everywhere else is pretty packed."* If they say yes, sit and eat. You don't have to force conversation right away. Just being there is step one.

At a club/team: *"Is this your first time at [club]? Mine too—kind of nervous!"* Or if they're veterans: *"You guys seem to know what you're doing. Any tips for a newbie?"*

In the hallway: *"I love your [thing]. Where'd you get it?"* Compliments are easy conversation starters.

At an event: *"This is so fun/weird/boring, right?"* Shared experiences = instant connection point.

Step-by-Step: What to Do If They Seem Closed Off

You tried to join, but they're giving you closed vibes. Don't panic. Here's how to exit gracefully:

1. Read the signals: Short answers, no eye contact, no questions back at you, physically turning away. These are clues.

2. Don't force it: If the vibe is off, acknowledge it internally and prepare to exit.

3. Exit with dignity: *"Cool, well, I'll let you guys get back to it. See you around!"* Keep it light and friendly.

4. Don't take it personally: Seriously. It's about group dynamics, not your worth. They might have inside drama, or they're just not in a welcoming mood.

5. Try again later (or don't): Sometimes timing is everything. You could try approaching them another day. Or, find a different group. Both options are valid.

Red Flags: When a Group Isn't Worth Your Time

Sometimes you get into a group and realize... wait, this isn't actually fun. Here are signs that a group isn't a good fit:

✖ You feel pressure to agree with everything they say, even when you don't

✖ You're constantly fake laughing or pretending to care about things

✖ They make fun of people (including you sometimes) and call it "joking"

✖ You feel like you're walking on eggshells around them

✖ They gossip constantly and you worry you'll be next

✖ They pressure you to do things you're uncomfortable with

✖ You feel worse about yourself after hanging out with them

If you're seeing these red flags, this isn't your crew. It's okay to slowly back away and find people who make you feel good, not stressed.

What to Say When You Feel Left Out

Let's talk about one of the worst feelings in middle school: being left out. Maybe your friends made plans without you. Maybe everyone's talking about something that happened and you weren't there. Maybe you're sitting alone while your usual group is somewhere else. It stings. Like, really stings.

First, let's validate that this is hard. Then, let's give you tools to handle it.

Real Talk: It Hurts to Feel Invisible

Here's what real middle schoolers said about feeling left out:

> "I walked into the cafeteria, and my usual table was full. Like, completely full. I stood there with my tray for what felt like forever before just... leaving and eating in the library. I cried in the bathroom after."
>
> — Jasmine, 7th grade

> "My friends had this whole inside joke from something that happened over the weekend. They kept laughing about it, and I had no idea what was going on. I felt like I wasn't even there."

— Eric, 6th grade

"I saw on Instagram that everyone hung out without me. They even posted pictures. Nobody said anything about it at school the next day, as if it never happened. That hurt more than anything."

— Maya, 8th grade

If this resonates with you, you're not alone. And it's not because you're unlikeable or boring or not good enough. Sometimes people are thoughtless. Sometimes plans happen randomly. Sometimes you get accidentally overlooked. It's not fair, but it happens to literally everyone.

Direct Scripts: What to Actually Say

When you're feeling left out, you have choices. Here are scripts for different situations:

Asking to join in the moment: "Hey, can I join you guys?" Keep it simple and direct. If they say yes, great. If they say they're saving seats or it's full, say "No worries, see you later" and move on with your dignity intact.

When they say they're saving a seat: Option 1: "Cool, who for?" (Sometimes it's a legit save.) Option 2: "Okay, no problem!" (Don't argue or guilt-trip. Just move on.)

When you weren't invited to plans: "Hey, I saw you guys hung out this weekend. Looked fun! How was it?" This lets them know you know, without accusing them. See how they respond. If they seem apologetic: "Next time, let me know if you're planning something!" If they brush it off or seem defensive, that tells you something about the friendship.

When you're consistently left out: "Hey, can we talk? I've noticed I haven't been included in stuff lately, and it's been bothering me. Is everything okay between us?" This is brave, but necessary. Real friends will hear you out.

Important: If you speak up and nothing changes, that's information. Maybe these aren't your people after all. It hurts, but it's better to know.

Solo Self-Care Moves When You're on Your Own

Sometimes you end up alone—whether by choice or circumstance. Here's how to make solo time less painful and maybe even... nice?

Put in headphones and listen to your favorite playlist: Music can be a mood shifter. Make a playlist specifically for tough days.

Sketch, doodle, or journal: Getting your feelings out on paper helps. Draw how you're feeling, write a rant, whatever works.

Organize something: Weird tip, but organizing your planner, backpack, or locker can make you feel more in control when other things feel chaotic.

Read something escapist: Get lost in a book, manga, fanfic—anything that takes you out of your current reality for a bit.

Text someone who gets it: A friend from a different school, a cousin, a sibling, someone from your old neighborhood. You don't have to be alone even if you're physically alone.

Treat yourself to something small: Buy that snack you love, watch a comfort show when you get home, or do something nice for yourself.

Challenge: Spot a Solo Sitter and Invite Them

Here's something powerful you can do: Remember how it feels to be left out? Use that to help someone else.

Look around your cafeteria or classroom. Is there someone sitting alone who looks like they could use a friendly face? Walk up and say:

"Hey, want to sit with me?"

"My table has room if you want to join us."

"I'm [your name]. Mind if I sit here?"

You might make someone's entire week. And bonus: You might make a real friend who knows what it's like to feel left out, too.

How to Bounce Back After Being Ghosted or Ignored

Ghosting isn't just a dating thing—it happens in friendships too. And it's confusing and hurtful. Let's talk about what it looks like, why it happens, and how to handle it without losing your mind.

What Ghosting Actually Looks Like

Ghosting can happen digitally or in real life. Here are examples:

Digital ghosting: They read your texts but don't respond. They're active on social media but don't reply to your DMs. They leave you on read for days (or forever). They stop reacting to your stories or posts.

In-person ghosting: They avoid eye contact in the hallway. They suddenly have "plans" every time you ask to hang out. They're friendly in class but disappear after school. They stop sitting with you at lunch without explanation.

Here's what makes ghosting extra hard: You don't know why. Did you do something wrong? Are they mad? Did they just forget? Are you being dramatic? The not-knowing is the worst part.

What to Do: The One-Text Rule

Here's a healthy boundary: Reach out ONCE. That's it. One check-in text. Then the ball is in their court.

Sample text: "Hey, haven't heard from you in a while. Everything okay?" or "Miss you! Want to catch up sometime?" or "Feels like we haven't talked in forever. Hope you're good!"

Then wait. If they respond, great. If they don't... that's your answer. Don't send a second text. Don't demand an explanation. Don't spiral into multiple messages. Just... let it go.

What NOT to Say

When you're hurt, it's tempting to send something angry or guilt-trippy. Don't. Here's what NOT to text:

✖ *"Wow, so you're just ignoring me now? Cool."*

✖ *"I guess our friendship meant nothing to you."*

✖ *"You're such a fake friend."*

✖ Twenty messages in a row asking *"hello??" "are you there??" "Answer me!"*

These texts feel good to send in the moment, but they make things worse. They come across as desperate or aggressive, even if you're just hurt. Keep your dignity.

Self-Care Checklist for Processing the Hurt

Being ghosted feels like rejection because... it kind of is. Here's how to take care of yourself:

Feel your feelings: It's okay to be sad, angry, confused, all of it. Don't pretend you're fine if you're not.

Talk to someone safe: A parent, sibling, friend from another group, or school counselor. Someone who will listen without judgment.

Write it out: Journal about what happened and how you feel. Getting it out of your head helps.

Don't check their social media obsessively: Seriously, this will make you feel worse. Mute or unfollow them if you need to.

Invest in other friendships: Spend time with people who DO text back, who DO show up. Don't put all your energy into someone who's ignoring you.

Remember it's not about your worth: People ghost for all kinds of reasons —they're overwhelmed, dealing with stuff, bad at communication, immature. Most of the time, it's not about you being "not good enough."

Moving Forward: List Two People You'd Like to Get to Know Better

Instead of fixating on the person who ghosted you, redirect your energy. Think of two classmates you'd like to get to know better and write them down:

1. Name: ____

Why I want to know them:

____

2. Name:

____

Why I want to know them:

____

Now make a plan to talk to at least one of them this week. A small conversation. A compliment. Anything.

When Your BFF Suddenly Changes—Handling Friendship Breakups

This might be the hardest part of middle school friendships: when your best friend suddenly feels like a stranger. Maybe they're hanging out with different people. Maybe they're into totally new things. Maybe they just... changed. And you're left wondering what happened to the person you used to know.

Here's the truth: Friendship breakups are real, they hurt as much as any other breakup, and they're incredibly common in middle school. Let's talk about why they happen and how to get through them.

Why Friendships Drift (And Why It's Usually Nobody's Fault)

Before you blame yourself—or them—understand that friendship shifts in middle school are normal. Here's why:

Different classes: You used to see each other all day. Now you're in different classes, different lunch periods, different schedules. You physically don't see each other as much.

New interests: They joined robotics and became obsessed with coding. You're all about art. Your worlds just... diverged. Neither interest is better or worse. They're just different.

Different friend groups: They found their people on the soccer team. You found yours in the drama club. You're still friends, but you're not each other's ONLY friend anymore.

Growth at different speeds: One of you is really into makeup and dating. The other still wants to play video games and avoid all that. You're maturing at different rates, and that's okay.

Drama or misunderstanding: Sometimes a fight or miscommunication creates a rift that never fully heals. The friendship becomes awkward instead of comfortable.

They moved or switched schools: Physical distance makes it hard to maintain friendships, even with technology.

The point? Most of the time, friendship drift isn't about one person being a bad friend. It's about change. And middle school is ALL about change.

"Closure Conversation" Scripts

Sometimes you need to talk about the elephant in the room. If you want closure, here's how to have that conversation:

In Person:

"Hey, can we talk for a sec? I feel like things have been different between us lately, and I miss how we used to be. Is everything okay?"

Then listen. Really listen. They might:

✓ Apologize and want to reconnect

✓ Admit they've been distant but didn't realize how it affected you

✓ Say they've changed and are into different things now

✓ Get defensive or dismissive (which tells you a lot)

Via Text (If In-Person Feels Too Hard):

"I've been thinking about our friendship lately, and it feels like things have changed. I miss hanging out like we used to. Can we talk about it?"

Keep it:

✓ Non-accusatory (use "I feel" not "You did")

✓ Honest but kind

✔ Open to their perspective

If they ignore you: If they don't respond or blow you off, that IS your answer. You tried. You can let go knowing you did your part.

Navigating Shared Spaces Post-Breakup

Here's the tricky part: You still see them. At school. In class. Maybe even in your friend group. How do you handle it without being weird or mean?

Be polite but not fake: You can say hi. You can be friendly. You don't have to pretend everything is fine, but you also don't need to be cold or dramatic.

Keep it surface-level: "Hey, how's it going?" "Good, you?" "Cool, see you around." That's enough. You don't owe them deep conversations.

Avoid trash-talking them: I know it's tempting, especially if you're hurt. But badmouthing them to mutual friends will make YOU look petty, not them.

Find new spots if needed: If seeing them at your usual lunch table is too much, find a new table. If they sit near you in class and it's awkward, ask the teacher if you can move (privately).

Focus on YOUR people: Invest in friendships that ARE working. Don't spend all your energy mourning this one friendship.

"What I Learned" Journal Template

Even when friendships end badly, you can learn from them. Use this template to reflect and grow:

WHAT I APPRECIATED about this friendship:

____

____

____

WHAT I WISH had been different:

____

____

____

WHAT I LEARNED about myself:

____

____

____

WHAT I WANT in future friendships:

____

____

____

One thing I would do differently next time:

____

This isn't about blaming yourself or them. It's about learning and moving forward.

Friendship "Glow Up" Tracker—Logging Wins and Learning from L's

Throughout this chapter, we've talked about making friends, joining groups, handling rejection, dealing with ghosting, and surviving breakups. That's a LOT. And it's easy to focus on the hard stuff and forget about the progress you're making.

That's why you need a Friendship Glow Up Tracker. This isn't just about celebrating wins—it's about learning from the awkward, messy, imperfect moments too. Because THAT'S where growth happens.

How to Use Your Friendship Tracker

Set aside 5-10 minutes at the end of each week to fill this out. Be honest. Be specific. This is for you, not for anyone else.

Friendship Glow Up Tracker Template

Copy this into a notebook, notes app, or print it out and fill it in weekly:

Week of: _____________________

AWKWARD MOMENT(S) THIS WEEK:

What happened? (be specific)

____

____

____

WHAT I TRIED:

What did I do to handle it? What script or strategy did I use?

____

____

____

WHAT HAPPENED:

How did it turn out? What was the result?

____

____

____

WHAT I LEARNED?

What would I do differently? What worked? What didn't?

____

____

____

FRIENDSHIP WIN THIS WEEK:

Even a small one! *(had a good conversation, made someone laugh, got invited somewhere, stood up for someone, etc)*

____

CONFIDENCE CHECK:

On a scale of 1-10 how confident do I feel in my friendships right now?

1 — 2 — 3 — 4 — 5 — 6 — 7 —8 — 9 — 10

Guided Reflection Questions (Use These Monthly)

1. Looking back at the past month, what patterns do I notice in my friendships?
2. What's one thing I'm doing better now than I was a month ago?
3. What's one social situation that used to scare me but no longer does?
4. Who are the people I feel most comfortable around? What do they have in common?
5. What's one thing I want to work on in the next month?

6. If I could give my past self one piece of friendship advice, what
    would it be?

Example Entry (So You Know What This Looks Like):

Week of: *October 15*

AWKWARD MOMENT: *I tried to join a group at lunch, and they kind of gave me cold vibes. I ended up sitting with them, but felt super awkward the whole time.*

WHAT I TRIED: *I used the script "Mind if I sit here?" They said okay, but didn't really include me in the conversation.*

WHAT HAPPENED: *It was uncomfortable. I finished lunch and left. Decided not to try that table again.*

WHAT I LEARNED: *Not every group is my group, and that's okay. I need to look for open vibes, not just any group.*

FRIENDSHIP WIN: *I had a really good conversation with someone in my art class about our favorite manga. They seem cool.*

CONFIDENCE CHECK: *6 - Not terrible, but not great. Still figuring things out.*

The Two-Week Challenge: Spot Your Biggest Glow Up

After you've filled out your tracker for two weeks, look back at your entries. Answer these questions:

1. What's one thing I did in week 2 that I wouldn't have done in
    week 1?
2. What social situation feels even a tiny bit easier now?
3. What's one script or strategy that actually worked for me?
4. How has my confidence changed? (Look at your confidence checks)
5. What's one thing I'm proud of myself for trying?

That's your glow up. It might not feel huge, but if you're even 1% braver, more confident, or more skilled at navigating friendships than you were two weeks ago? That's growth. That's success. Keep going.

Friendships Are Messy—And That's Okay

If there's one thing I want you to take away from this chapter, it's this: Friendship in middle school is complicated. It's not like elementary school, where you're friends with whoever lives on your street or sits at your table. You're figuring out who you are, what you value, and who your real people are. That takes time. That takes mistakes. That takes awkward moments, hurt feelings, and do-overs.

But here's what else is true: You are worthy of real friendship. The kind where people text back. Where you don't have to pretend to be someone you're not. Where you feel seen and valued. Those friendships exist, and you will find them. Keep putting yourself out there. Keep being kind. Keep tracking your growth. You're doing better than you think.

three
drama-proofing your social life--- gossip, rumors, and group chats

Welcome to the messiest chapter in this book. We're talking about drama---the kind that starts with 'Did you hear...?' and ends with half the grade being involved in something that started over literally nothing.

Here's the reality: Middle school drama is inevitable. Someone will spread a rumor. Someone will screenshot a private message. Someone will start something in a group chat that spirals out of control. You can't completely avoid it. But you CAN learn how to handle it, protect yourself, and — most importantly — avoid making it worse.

Let's get into it.

Friendship Drama Decoder---Gossip, Rumors, and "Did You Hear...?"

Gossip and rumors spread through middle school like wildfire. One person says something to one person, who tells two people, who each tell three people, and by lunchtime, the entire school 'knows' something that might not even be true.

How Rumors Actually Spread: The Flowchart

Here's the typical path a rumor takes:

STEP 1: The Spark

Someone sees, hears, or makes up something about someone else. Maybe it's true, maybe it's exaggerated, maybe it's completely false.

↓

STEP 2: The First Tell

They tell their "closest friend" in confidence. "Don't tell anyone, but..." (Spoiler: Their friend will definitely tell someone.)

↓

STEP 3: The Spread

That friend tells 2-3 people. Each of them tells 2-3 people. Each retelling adds details, removes context, or changes the story.

↓

STEP 4: The Group Chat

Someone brings it up in a group chat. Now 20+ people know. Screenshots start happening. People who weren't even there are now "experts."

↓

STEP 5: Peak Drama

The person the rumor is about finds out. They're hurt, angry, and confused. Sides are taken. Friend groups split.

↓

STEP 6: The Aftermath

Either the truth comes out, and people feel guilty, OR the rumor fades, but damage is done, OR adults have to intervene.

↓

Why Do People Gossip?

To feel important: "I know something you don't" makes people feel powerful.

To fit in: If everyone's talking about it, staying silent feels like being left out.

Boredom: Gossip fills conversational voids.

Jealousy or resentment: Spreading rumors feels like a form of revenge.

They think it's true: They heard it from someone they trust and didn't question it.

"Magic Phrases" to Stop Gossip in Its Tracks

You have more power than you think to shut down gossip:

"That sounds sus---maybe we should check before spreading that." Plants doubt without being preachy.

"I don't know if that's true, so I'm not going to repeat it." Takes you out of the rumor chain.

"That's not really my business." --- Polite way of saying "not getting involved."

"I don't feel comfortable talking about someone who's not here." Mature and hard to argue with.

"Can we talk about something else?" Direct subject change.

Pro tip: You don't have to lecture people. Just refusing to participate is enough. Most gossip dies when people stop feeding it.

Real Stories: Long-Term Impact

Regret: "I spread a rumor about someone in seventh grade because I was mad. It got huge. They switched schools. I still feel terrible three years later." - Anonymous, 10th grade

Repair: "Someone said I cheated on a test. It wasn't true. I had to prove it to the teacher. It was humiliating. I forgave them eventually, but we're not friends anymore." - Kai, 8th grade

Moving On: "There was a rumor I was dating someone I wasn't. I ignored it. People got bored after two weeks." - Taylor, 7th grade

Rumor Control---What to Do When the Tea Is About You

So you've heard there's a rumor about you. Your stomach drops. Your face gets hot. You feel exposed and powerless. Take a breath. This is manageable. Here's your step-by-step plan.

Step 1: Recognize and Manage Your Initial Emotional Response

First, acknowledge what you're feeling:

☐ Shocked or blindsided

☐ Angry at whoever started it

☐ Hurt that people believe it

☐ Embarrassed (even if it's not true)

☐ Scared about what people think

☐ Wanting to lash out immediately

What NOT to do in the first hour:

✖ Fire off angry texts to everyone

✖ Post a defensive rant on social media

✖ Confront someone publicly in the cafeteria

✖ Spread a counter-rumor

Instead, give yourself time to calm down. Go for a walk. Text a trusted friend or parent. Cry if you need to. Process the emotion

before you respond.

Step 2: Scripts for Confronting Calmly

If you want to address it, here's how:

"Hey, can we talk privately? I heard you said something specific about me. Can you tell me what happened?"

This script is:

☑ Calm, not accusatory

☑ Asks for their side

☑ Specific (not vague)

☑ Private (not in front of others)

Possible outcomes:

✓ They apologize → Accept it, but set boundaries

✓ They deny it or blame someone else → *"Okay, I wanted to hear your side. Just know it's been hurtful."*

✓ They get defensive or mean → Walk away. You tried.

Step 3: The Ignore vs. Confront Decision Tree

Use this to decide your response:

Is the rumor causing real harm?

→ YES: Address it

→ NO: Consider ignoring it

Do people actually believe it?

→ YES: You may need to clarify

→ NO: Let it fizzle out

Is it based on truth, but exaggerated?

→ YES: Set the record straight

→ NO (completely false): Deny it clearly once

Step 4: Template for Explaining to Trusted Adults

"I need help with a situation. There's a rumor going around about me that [brief description]. I've tried what you've done, but it's not stopping, and it's affecting friendships/focus/safety. I have screenshots/evidence if that helps. What can we do?"

Pro tip: Bring screenshots or other evidence if you have it. This helps adults take action.

Step 5: The "No Cap" Statement Exercise

Ground yourself in truth:

What the rumor says:

____

____

What I KNOW is true about myself:

____

____

People who know the real me:

____

____

How I want to respond:

____

The Group Chat Code---Joining, Surviving, and Avoiding Ghosting

Group chats are where a lot of middle school life happens. Planning hangouts, sharing memes, doing homework together---and sometimes drama. Let's talk about navigating them.

Group Chat Etiquette 101

How to Ask to Join:

"Hey, do you guys have a group chat for a project/club? Mind if I join?"

"Can you add me to the group chat? I keep missing out on plans!"

"Is there a class group chat for homework help?"

DO'S and DON'Ts for Adding People:

✓ DO ask the group before adding someone

✓ DO add people relevant to the chat's purpose

✗ DON'T add people without permission

✗ DON'T add people to stir drama

✗ DON'T create a chat about someone without them in it

Unspoken Rules Everyone Should Know

Reply timing: You don't have to respond instantly, but totally ignoring an active conversation reads as rude. If you need a break, mute the chat.

Inside jokes: A few are fun. If EVERY message is an inside joke, you're excluding people.

Don't spam: 47 messages in a row? Combine your thoughts.

Read the room: Match the energy. Don't drop memes during serious conversations.

FOMO is real: If planning hangouts, invite everyone in the chat OR move to DMs.

How to Exit Gracefully

MUTE: Silent in settings. No announcement needed. Perfect when it's too active.

ARCHIVE: Disappears from the main list, but you're still in it. Silent.

LEAVE (casual chat): *"Hey everyone, too many notifications, so I'm leaving this chat. See you at school!"*

LEAVE (close friends): *"Hey guys, need a break from group chats. Not personal, just need phone space. Will text individually!"*

Remember: You don't need permission to leave. If it's stressing you out, you can leave. Your mental health > FOMO.

Group Chat Drama Decoder---Surviving Digital Exclusion

Digital exclusion -> being left out of group chats, ignored in existing chats, or watching plans unfold without you is painful. You can see exactly how much you're being excluded.

Green Flags vs. Red Flags in Group Chats

✓ GREEN FLAG CHATS:

☑ People respond to everyone (not just certain people)

☑ Topics are inclusive

☑ If plans are made, everyone is invited, or it moves to DMs

☑ Jokes are funny to everyone

☑ People are supportive

☑ Mistakes are addressed kindly

✗ RED FLAG CHATS:

🚫 Only certain people get responses

🚫 Lots of inside jokes that exclude people

🚫 Plans made in chat, but not everyone was invited

🚫 People mocked and told, "It's just a joke."

🚫 Screenshots shared without permission

🚫 Clear hierarchy of who matters

🚫 You feel worse after reading

Scripts for Responding to Being Left Out

Direct Check-In: *"Hey, I feel like I've been left out lately. Did I miss something?"*

Specific Call-Out: *"Plans were made, and I wasn't invited. Is there a reason?"*

Exit Script: *"This chat doesn't feel like my vibe. I'm going to leave, but no hard feelings!"*

Starting Your Own Positive Group Chat

Pick your people: 3-5 people who are kind and fun.

Give it a purpose: Homework help, memes, a specific interest, or just friends talking.

Set the vibe early: First messages set the tone. Keep it positive.

Make everyone matter: Respond to everyone. No one should feel invisible.

Handle issues quickly: *"Let's keep this positive,"* or *"That was mean, can we not?"*

Challenge: One Week Without the Toxic Chat

Experiment: Mute or leave for one week. Journal about:

☐ Do I feel less stressed?

☐ Am I checking my phone less?

☐ Do I feel less FOMO?

☐ Am I happier?

☐ Do I actually miss it?

After a week, decide: Go back, or is life better without it?

How to Exit a Toxic Group (IRL or Online) Without Being Salty

Sometimes you realize a group, whether a friend group, club, team, or chat, is actually toxic. It's making you miserable. Here's how to get out with dignity.

Checklist: Is This Group Toxic?

Check all that apply:

☐ Constant negativity and complaining

☐ People are excluded regularly (including you)

☐ Peer pressure to do things you're uncomfortable with

☐ You're mocked or criticized, then told "it's just a joke."

☐ Drama is constant---every day there's a new crisis

☐ You feel like you're walking on eggshells

☐ Your values don't align with the group's behavior

☐ You feel worse about yourself after hanging with them

☐ You dread seeing notifications from this group

If you checked 3 or more, this group might not be good for you.

Exit Scripts That Maintain Your Dignity

For online groups: *"I need a break from this chat---see you around!"* Short, no explanation needed.

For IRL groups (slow fade): Gradually decline invitations. *"Can't make it this time." "Have plans already."* Eventually, stop being invited. No confrontation needed.

For IRL groups (direct): *"Hey, I think I need some space. It's not personal, I just need to focus on other things right now."*

Handling Pushback

They might not let you go quietly. Here's what to expect and how to respond:

They guilt-trip: *"Wow, so you're just abandoning us?"* → *"I need to do what's best for me right now."*

They spread rumors: Let them. Your real friends will ask you directly. Don't engage or defend.

They try to pull you back in: *"We miss you! Come back!"* → *"I appreciate that, but I'm good where I'm at."*

Pro tip: Don't announce a dramatic exit or post about it. Don't trash-talk them publicly. Just quietly remove yourself. Less drama = cleaner break.

Self-Care Post-Exit

After leaving a toxic group, you might feel:

✔ Relief (finally!)

✔ Guilt (am I being mean?)

✔ Loneliness (even if they were toxic, they were familiar)

✔ Freedom (I can be myself now)

All normal. Here's how to fill the void:

- Join healthier groups: Clubs, teams, volunteer work. Find YOUR people.
- Focus on hobbies: Art, music, sports, reading---whatever makes you happy.
- Reconnect with old friends: People you drifted from when you were in the toxic group.
- Give yourself grace: It takes time to find your people. You did the right thing.

Rebuilding Trust After Drama---Real Steps, Not Just "Be Nice"

So drama happened. Maybe you were part of it. Maybe you were the victim. Maybe you were a bystander who got caught up. Now you want to fix things and rebuild trust. Here's the truth: 'Just apologize and move on' isn't enough. Trust is rebuilt through consistent action over time. Let's break down how.

Why Trust Breaks Down (And Why "Sorry" Isn't Magic)

Trust breaks when:

- Someone breaks a promise or commitment
- Secrets are shared or screenshot without permission

- People lie or manipulate
- Someone is excluded or ghosted without explanation
- Hurtful things are said (even "as a joke")
- Apologies are given, but behavior doesn't change

A simple 'sorry' doesn't fix these. Why? Because trust is about believing someone's ACTIONS will match their words. If you say sorry but keep doing the hurtful thing, the apology means nothing.

The Real Apology Script: Taking Responsibility

A real apology has four parts:

1. Acknowledge what you did (specifically)

2. Take responsibility (no excuses)

3. Express understanding of how it affected them

4. Explain what you'll do differently

Example: "I'm sorry I [specific action]. I know that was wrong, and there's no excuse for it. I understand it made you feel hurt/excluded/betrayed, and that makes sense. Going forward, I'm going to [specific change in behavior]. Can we talk about how to move forward?"

What a Bad Apology Looks Like (Avoid These):

"I'm sorry you feel that way." → This isn't an apology, it's dismissive

"I'm sorry, BUT you also…" → The "but" cancels out the apology

"I already said sorry, what more do you want?" → Apologies aren't checkboxes

"Sorry if I hurt you." → "If?" Either you did, or you didn't

The Patience Timeline: Trust Takes Time

After a genuine apology, understand:

Week 1-2: They're watching to see if you mean it. Your actions matter more than words.

Week 3-4: Small signs of trust returning. They might test you and give you a small piece of information to see if you keep it private.

Month 2-3: Friendship feels more comfortable again, but they're still a little guarded.

Month 4+: If you've been consistent, trust can be fully rebuilt. Some friendships end up stronger.

Important: This timeline assumes consistent positive behavior. If you mess up again, you start over---or the friendship ends. Second chances are gifts, not guarantees.

Setting Boundaries During Rebuilding

If you're the one who was hurt, you can rebuild trust while protecting yourself:

"I accept your apology, but I need some space before we hang out again."

"I'm willing to give this another chance, but if specific behavior happens again, I'm done."

"We can be friendly at school, but I'm not ready for group chats or hangouts yet."

Boundaries aren't mean. They're self-protection while you see if the person has really changed.

Reflection: What Did I Learn?

Whether you were the person who messed up or the person who was hurt, take time to reflect:

What happened, specifically?

____

____

____

What was my role in this? (Even if small)

____

____

____

What did I learn about myself?

____

____

____

What did I learn about friendships?

____

____

What will I do differently next time?

____

____

____

How do I want to show up in relationships going forward?

____

____

____

Drama is painful, but it can teach you a lot about what you value, what you won't tolerate, and how you want to treat people.

You're More Drama-Proof Than You Think

Here's what you now know how to do:

✓ Shut down gossip before it spreads

✓ Handle rumors about you with dignity

✓ Navigate group chats without losing your mind

✓ Recognize and leave toxic groups

✓ Rebuild trust when friendships break

Middle school drama is messy, complicated, and sometimes unavoidable. But you don't have to be a victim of it or a participant in making it worse. You now have scripts, strategies, and boundaries. Use them.

Remember: Your peace matters more than being included in every group. Your integrity matters more than being popular. Your real friends will respect your boundaries and won't make you choose between your values and your social life.

four
bully-proof—
standing up without
standing out

There's a difference between a bad day and bullying. There's a difference between someone being annoying and someone targeting you. And there's a big difference between normal middle school conflict—the kind where feelings get hurt, people say dumb things, and everyone moves on—and the kind of repeated, intentional behavior that makes you dread going to school.

This chapter is about that second kind. We're going to talk about how to recognize it, how to respond to it, how to handle it when it goes digital, and what to do when the adults around you aren't helping the way they should. Because you deserve to feel safe at school. Full stop.

Spot the Signs—Is It Bullying or Just Annoying?

Before we dive into strategies, let's get clear on what bullying actually is—because there's a lot of confusion about this, and that confusion can make it harder to get help.

The Big Difference: Conflict vs. Bullying

Not every mean thing someone does is bullying. That matters, because the response is different depending on which one you're dealing with.

Normal conflict looks like this:

✓ Two people disagree and both feel upset

✓ It happens once or occasionally, not constantly

✓ Both people have roughly equal power in the situation

✓ It can usually be resolved with a conversation

✓ Neither person feels genuinely afraid of the other

Bullying looks like this:

! One person repeatedly targets another

! There's a power imbalance — physical size, social status, group vs. individual

! The target feels afraid, humiliated, or unsafe

! It keeps happening even after the target has asked for it to stop

! The person doing it seems to enjoy the reaction or the control

> "They always joke about my shoes. Every single day. I've told them it's not funny but they keep doing it. My friends say to ignore it, but it doesn't stop. It just feels like I can't escape it."
>
> — Jaylen, 6th grade

> "Someone called me a name once in the hallway. It hurt, but it didn't happen again. That was just a bad day, not bullying. I know the difference now."
>
> — Sofia, 7th grade

The Four Types of Bullying

1. Verbal Bullying: Name-calling, insults, threats, or humiliating comments —whether in person or in writing. This includes "just joking" comments that consistently target the same person.

2. Physical Bullying: Hitting, pushing, tripping, or deliberately damaging someone's stuff. This is the most visible type, but not the most common in middle school.

3. Social/Relational Bullying: Excluding someone on purpose, spreading rumors, turning people against someone, or manipulating friendships to hurt someone. This type is sneaky, often denied as "just drama," and can be the most emotionally damaging.

4. Cyberbullying: Bullying that happens through phones, apps, games, or social media. More on this in its own section below, because it comes with its own set of complications.

· · ·

"IS IT BULLYING?" Flowchart

START: Did someone do or say something that hurt you?

↓

Has it happened more than once?

NO → Probably a conflict or a bad moment. Try addressing it directly or letting it go.

YES → Keep going.

↓

Is there a power imbalance? (They're bigger, more popular, in a group while you're alone, etc.)

NO → Still hurtful conflict. Use communication strategies.

YES → Keep going.

↓

Have you asked them to stop (or made it clear that it bothers you), and it still continues?

NO → Try assertive communication first (see next section).

YES → This is likely bullying. You deserve adult support.

Trust Your Gut

Here's a simple rule: If something keeps happening, it keeps hurting you, and you've tried to make it stop but can't, that is not something you should have to handle alone. Trust how you feel. Your discomfort is information, not weakness.

Glow Up Tracker Prompt: If something has been bothering you, write it down. Date, what happened, who was involved. Tracking patterns helps you see if it's a one-time thing or something more serious.

What to Actually Say -"Magic Phrases" for Shutting Down Bullies and Bystanders

You don't have to have a perfectly crafted speech ready. What matters most is that you respond in a way that doesn't reward the bully (attention, a reaction, escalation) while still protecting your dignity. Here's your toolkit.

THE MAGIC PHRASE Chart

FOR VERBAL BULLYING (name-calling, insults, put-downs):

"Not cool. Stop." — Simple, direct, no argument needed.

"That's not funny to me." — Calm, factual, doesn't escalate.

"Okay." — No reaction. No fuel for the fire. Just "okay" and walk away.

"Thanks for your opinion." — Disarms them because it's not what they expected.

"Why would you say that?" — Makes them explain themselves. Awkward for them, not you.

FOR SOCIAL BULLYING (exclusion, rumors, manipulation):

"You can include or exclude whoever you want, but I'm not going to pretend that's okay."

"I heard what was said. That's not true, and I'm not going to engage with it."

"If you have a problem with me, tell me directly. I'm right here."

FOR "JUST JOKING" SITUATIONS:

"I get that you think it's a joke, but it doesn't feel funny to me. Please stop."

"You've said that a few times now. It's not something I find funny. Can we move on?"

"Jokes are supposed to make everyone laugh. This one doesn't land for me."

FOR BYSTANDERS (when someone else is being targeted):

"Hey, that's not cool." — Short and simple. Shifts the group energy.

"Leave them alone." — Direct, no drama.

"Hey [target's name], want to walk to class together?" — Removes them from the situation without confrontation.

"I'm going to get a teacher if this keeps up." — A warning that shows you mean business.

Body Language That Says "I'm Not a Target"

You don't have to feel confident to look confident. Your body language sends a message before you even open your mouth. Here's what confident looks like—even when your heart is pounding:

- **Stand tall.** Shoulders back, not hunched. You're taking up your space in the world, and that's fine.

- **Eye contact.** Not a staring contest—just steady, calm eye contact. Looking at the floor signals that you're shrinking. You don't have to shrink.
- **Keep your voice even.** Not loud, not shaky. Calm and flat. Practice if you need to.
- **Hands relaxed.** Crossed arms look defensive. Fists look aggressive. Hands loose at your sides = neutral and calm.
- **Walk away with purpose.** If you choose to leave, leave like you meant to do that. Not running. Not storming off. Just walking.

> "I used to look at the floor whenever someone said something mean to me. My school counselor told me to just look up, make eye contact, and say nothing. I tried it. It was so hard the first time, but it actually worked. They kind of didn't know what to do with that." — Mia, 7th grade

When to Walk Away (And When Walking Away Isn't Enough)

Sometimes the best response is no response—you look at them calmly, you turn around, and you leave. This works especially well when:

1. The bully is looking for a big emotional reaction
2. You're outnumbered, and engaging would escalate things
3. You feel unsafe
4. You've already said something, and they're not stopping

But walking away is NOT enough when:

1. It's physical, and your safety is at risk
2. It's happening repeatedly, and walking away hasn't made it stop
3. It involves threats, online harassment, or screenshots being spread
4. Other people are being hurt too

In those cases, walking away is still the right move in the moment—but it's not the only step. You also need to loop in an adult.

Script for getting a peer to back you up: *"Hey, can you walk with me to class? That situation back there was making me uncomfortable, and I don't want to be alone right now."*

WHAT TO DO When Bullying Goes Digital—Screenshots, Privacy, and Getting Help

Cyberbullying is bullying that happens through technology—phones, apps, social media, gaming platforms, or any other digital space. And it comes with a unique set of challenges that in-person bullying doesn't have.

Why Cyberbullying Hits Different

It follows you home. In-person bullying mostly happens at school. Cyberbullying is in your pocket 24/7.

There's an audience. A mean comment in a group chat can be seen by 20, 50, or hundreds of people instantly.

There's a record. Screenshots last forever. What gets posted or sent doesn't just disappear.

It can be anonymous. Fake accounts, anonymous apps, and throwaway usernames make it easier for bullies to hide.

The target is more isolated. You're facing it alone, on a screen, often at night when you can't easily talk to someone.

> "Someone made a fake account with my photos and started posting mean stuff pretending to be me. I didn't even know about it for two weeks. By the time I found out, people I didn't know were commenting on it. It was the scariest thing that's ever happened to me online." — Anonymous, 8th grade

Cyberbullying: Where It Happens

Group chats: Mean comments, being left out, being talked about in chats you're excluded from

Social media: Negative comments, mean DMs, fake accounts, unflattering photos posted without permission

Gaming platforms: Targeted harassment in games, being kicked out of groups, trash talk that goes too far

Anonymous apps: Apps specifically designed to allow anonymous messages —these are a hotspot for cruelty

Email and texting: Direct messages designed to threaten, harass, or intimidate

Step-by-Step: Documenting Digital Bullying

If you're experiencing cyberbullying, documentation is your power. Here's exactly what to do:

Step 1: Screenshot Everything

Screenshot every message, post, comment, or image that is hurtful, threatening, or harassing. Even if you think it's minor. Capture the username, the timestamp, and the content.

Step 2: Save to a Separate Folder

Create a folder on your phone or computer labeled something neutral (not visible on your lock screen). Date each screenshot as you save it: "10.14 — group chat — mean comment."

Step 3: Record the Details

In a notes app or notebook, write down: username of the person involved, platform, date and time, what was said or done, and any witnesses.

Step 4: Don't Delete the Originals Yet

Even if you want to delete the app or the messages, hold off until an adult has helped you use the evidence. Deleting first removes your proof.

Step 5: Tell a Trusted Adult

Bring your documentation. Walk them through it. (More on this in the next section.)

What NOT to Do When You're Being Cyberbullied

When you're hurt and angry, your instincts might tell you to:

🚫 **Fire back.** Don't. Even if you have the perfect clapback. Responding gives them what they want (a reaction) and can escalate things fast.

🚫 **Post about it publicly.** This fuels drama, invites more people into the situation, and can sometimes get you in trouble too.

🚫 **Share their information in retaliation.** This is never okay and can cross into illegal territory.

🚫 **Delete all the evidence.** You need it. Save first, delete later if you choose.

🚫 **Convince yourself it'll stop on its own.** Sometimes it does. But if it's repeated and intentional, it usually doesn't stop without intervention.

When Adults Don't Listen—How to Get Heard

You told an adult. Maybe it was a teacher. Maybe a parent or a counselor. And they said something like: "Just ignore them and they'll stop." Or "Kids will be kids." Or "Try to be nicer to them."

And you stood there thinking: That is not helpful at all.

First: That frustration is completely valid. Adults don't always get it right the first time. Second: You have the right to keep trying until someone takes action. Here's how.

> "My teacher said 'just ignore them and they'll stop.' I had been ignoring them for two months. It wasn't stopping. I had to go to the counselor instead." — DeAndre, 7th grade

How to Find the Right Adult Ally

Not every adult will be the right fit. Here's what to look for:

✓ **They actually listen** without cutting you off or rushing to give advice

✓ **They take you seriously** instead of minimizing or dismissing

✓ **They keep things private** unless they're legally required to act

✓ **They follow through** — they do what they say they'll do

✓ **They ask questions** instead of just telling you what to feel or do

Good options to try:

- School counselor
- A favorite teacher (not necessarily the one in whose class it's happening)
- A parent, guardian, or trusted family member
- School principal or assistant principal (if counselor doesn't act)
- A coach, club advisor, or other trusted adult

How to Present Your Case Effectively

Before you go to an adult, gather your thoughts. Be specific. Here's a template:

Your script: *"I need help with something that's been happening for [how long]. [Specific person or group] has been [specific behavior] on [specific occasions]. I've tried [what you've already done], but it hasn't stopped. It's affecting [my ability to focus / my friendships / how safe I feel at school]. I have [evidence/documentation/names of witnesses] if that helps. I need help figuring out what to do next."*

This script works because it:

- Is specific, not vague ("bullying" is easier to dismiss than "this specific thing that happened on these specific days")
- Shows you've tried to handle it yourself
- Explains the real-world impact
- Comes with evidence
- Asks for help without demanding a specific outcome

What To Do If the First Adult Doesn't Help

Try again with more detail:

"I brought this to you on [date] and it's still happening. Here's what's occurred since then. Can we come up with an actual plan?"

Go to someone else:

You are not limited to one person. If a teacher brushes you off, go to the counselor. If the counselor dismisses it, go to the principal. If school staff aren't helping, talk to a parent about reaching out to the school directly.

Put it in writing:

"Hi [name], I wanted to follow up in writing because I've been dealing with a bullying situation and I want to make sure it's formally on record. I spoke to [person] on [date] about [brief description]. Here's what has happened since then. I'm asking for [specific action]. Thank you."

Know your rights:

Schools are required by law to address bullying, especially when it involves harassment based on race, gender, disability, or other protected characteristics. If a school is failing to act, parents can escalate to the school district.

Important reminder: Asking for help isn't being dramatic. It's being smart. The people who are the best at self-advocacy are the ones who learned to keep trying until someone listened. You're learning that skill right now.

Being a Bystander—The Power of Stepping In

Here's something that doesn't get talked about enough: Most bullying happens in front of other people. And most of those people do nothing. Not because they're bad people—but because they don't know what to do, they're afraid of becoming the next target, or they assume someone else will step in.

But here's what research shows: When even ONE person speaks up or steps in, bullying stops or reduces significantly. One person. That person could be you.

Types of Bystanders

The Passive Bystander

Watches but does nothing. Doesn't want trouble, feels frozen, or tells themselves it's not their problem. This is the most common type—and honestly, the most understandable one. But silence can feel like approval to both the bully and the target.

The Reinforcing Bystander

Laughs, cheers, or encourages the bully (even just by watching and smiling). May not realize they're making it worse, but they are.

The Active Bystander

Steps in. This doesn't have to mean confronting the bully directly—it means doing something. Anything. Here's how:

Bystander Moves That Actually Work

The Distraction:

"Hey [target's name], didn't you say you were looking for the gym? I'll walk with you."

You're not confronting the bully. You're just removing the target from the situation. Clean, low-risk, effective.

The Direct Call-Out:

"Hey, that's not cool. Cut it out."

Simple. Short. Shifts the energy in the room. Most effective when done calmly, not aggressively.

The Recruit:

If you don't feel safe acting alone, find another bystander and ask them to act with you. Two people speaking up carries double the weight.

The Later Check-In:

"Hey, I saw what happened back there. Are you okay? That wasn't okay."

Even if you couldn't act in the moment, letting the target know someone saw it and cares matters enormously.

THE REPORT

Go to an adult. You don't have to use the target's name if you're not sure they want you to—you can just say what you witnessed and ask the adult to check in.

> "Someone in my class was always getting picked on at lunch. One day I just sat next to them. I didn't say anything about what was happening, just started talking to them like normal. The group doing it kind of drifted away. Sometimes you don't have to make a big speech. You just have to show up." — Priya, 8th grade

What About When You're Afraid?

Being scared of becoming a target yourself is a real fear. Here's the truth: Most bullies are looking for easy targets—people who are alone, who won't speak up, who don't have backup. A person with friends, confidence, and a willingness to call things out is not usually who they go after.

That said, you should never put yourself in physical danger. If the situation feels unsafe, your job is to get an adult—not to be a hero. Being a bystander doesn't mean risking your own safety. It means doing whatever you CAN safely do.

If YOU Have Bullied Someone—A Real Conversation

Most bullying chapters talk exclusively to the target. But here's the thing: Sometimes good people do hurtful things without fully realizing what they're doing. Sometimes you join in on teasing because everyone else is. Sometimes you exclude someone without thinking about how it feels to them. Sometimes you say something "as a joke" that lands differently than you intended.

If any part of this chapter made you wince because you recognized yourself on the other side, that matters. That discomfort is your conscience, and it's a good thing.

Honest Questions to Ask Yourself

☐ Have I said or done things repeatedly that I knew made someone uncomfortable?

☐ Have I joined in on teasing or mocking someone to fit in?

☐ Have I excluded someone intentionally or helped spread rumors?

☐ Have I sent messages or posted things online that were meant to hurt?

☐ Have I told someone "it's just a joke" when I actually knew it bothered them?

If you checked any of these honestly, it doesn't make you a terrible person. It makes you a person who has some work to do. Here's where to start:

• **Acknowledge it to yourself.** Without excuses. Without "but they…" Just: I did something hurtful.

• **Apologize — really apologize.** Use the four-part apology format from Chapter 3. Own what you did, understand the impact, and explain what you'll do differently.

• **Change the behavior.** The apology means nothing without the change. This is the hard part, and also the most important part.

• **Talk to someone.** A counselor, a trusted adult, a parent — not to get in trouble, but to understand why it happened and how to do better.

> "I was part of a group that was mean to this one kid all of seventh grade. I never said the worst stuff, but I laughed. One day, I realized he had basically stopped talking in class. Stopped participating in anything. I apologized to him the next year. He said he appreciated it. I still think about it."
>
> — Anonymous, 9th grade

The Bully-Proof Glow Up Tracker

Whether you've been navigating bullying yourself, being a bystander, or just learning how to handle tough situations with more confidence, this tracker is your space to reflect and grow.

Week of:

____

SITUATION THIS WEEK:

Describe what happened (bullying, bystander moment, or a tough conflict):

____

____

____

WHAT I DID:

How did I respond? What phrase or strategy did I use (or wish I had used)?

____

____

____

WHAT HAPPENED:

How did it turn out?

____

____

____

WHAT I LEARNED:

What would I do the same? What would I try differently?

____

____

____

MY CONFIDENCE CHECK:

How confident did I feel standing up for myself or others this week?

1 ---- 2 ---- 3 ---- 4 ---- 5 ---- 6 ---- 7 ---- 8 ---- 9 ---- 10

ONE THING I'M PROUD OF THIS WEEK (even small):

____

Monthly Reflection

1. When did I feel most in control of a tough situation this month?

2. What's one phrase I've actually used that worked?

3. What's one situation I handled differently than I would have a month ago?

4. Is there someone I want to check in on who might be dealing with this?

You're More Bully-Proof Than You Think

Here's what you now know how to do:

- Tell the difference between normal conflict and actual bullying

• Respond with phrases that protect your dignity without escalating

• Use your body language to show calm confidence even when you don't feel it

• Document cyberbullying and protect yourself online

• Get your story heard by adults—even when the first one doesn't listen

• Be the bystander who steps in instead of looking away

• Recognize if you've caused harm—and know what to do about it

Being bully-proof doesn't mean nothing can ever hurt you. It means you have tools, you know your worth, and you know how to take action instead of just hoping things get better.

That's a big deal.

five

organization hacks —no more lost homework or missed deadlines

L et's be real for a second: Middle school is a lot. You're juggling six or seven different teachers, each with their own expectations, deadlines, and grading styles. You have homework from multiple classes, sometimes all due on the same day. You have tests to study for, projects to plan, and forms your parents need to sign before tomorrow morning. Oh, and you also have, you know, a life.

The students who thrive in middle school aren't necessarily the smartest ones. They're the organized ones. The ones who have a system. And here's the best news: Organization is a skill, not a personality trait. You can learn it. You can build it. And once you have it, everything else gets easier.

This chapter will show you how.

> "I used to lose homework constantly. Not because I didn't do it—because I did it and then couldn't find it. My binder was a disaster. Once I set up a color system, it was like a totally different experience. I actually started turning stuff in on time."
>
> — Keisha, 7th grade

Color-Coding Your Life—Planners, Binders, and Digital Apps That Actually Work

Color-coding sounds like something your super-organized older sibling does. But here's the thing: it works for everyone, including people who consider themselves hopeless at organization. Your brain is wired to process color faster than words. When everything has a color, you stop having to think—you just see it and go.

The Color-Code System: Set It Up Once, Use It All Year

Pick one color per subject and stick to it ALL year—folder, notebook, planner tab, phone calendar. Everything for that subject = that color. Here's a sample setup:

- **Math:** Blue — it's cool and logical, just like numbers (debatable, but go with it)

- **Science:** Green — nature, experiments, living things

- **English/Language Arts:** Red — red pen edits, writing, words

- **Social Studies/History:** Orange — warm, earthy, old maps

- **Electives (Art, Music, PE, etc.):** Purple — creative and flexible

- **Homeroom/Advisory/Everything Else:** Yellow — bright and catch-all

You don't have to use these exact colors. Pick what feels right to you. The only rule: one color per subject, and keep it consistent.

Color-Coding Within Each Physical Binder

You've got two options for how to set up your binder:

Option A: One Big Binder with Dividers

Get a 2-inch binder and colored dividers (one per subject). Behind each divider: class notes in front, handouts in the middle, completed homework in the back. This keeps everything in one place—great if you tend to lose individual folders.

Option B: Individual Subject Folders

A separate folder for each subject in that subject's color. Left pocket: stuff to do or turn in. Right pocket: stuff that's done or you need to keep. This is lighter to carry but requires you to grab the right folder each day.

   Pro tip: Whatever system you pick, add a "homework due" pocket to each folder. Before you leave class, anything due soon goes directly into that pocket. No more searching.

The Emergency Supply Pocket

Inside the front cover of your binder or in a pencil pouch, keep:

- ☐ 3 pens (at least two different colors)

- ☐ 3 pencils and a small eraser

☐ A highlighter (or two)

☐ 5-6 sticky notes

☐ A few index cards

☐ A small ruler

☐ One spare hair tie (trust me)

Restock this whenever it runs low. Being the person who always has a pen = instant friend points.

Digital Color-Coding: Google Calendar and Apps

If you prefer going digital, color-coding works just as well on your phone or laptop:

Google Calendar:

- Create a separate calendar for each subject
- Assign each subject calendar its color
- Add assignment due dates, test dates, and project deadlines as events
- Turn on notifications for 1 day before and 1 hour before each deadline
- Check it every Sunday to see the week ahead

Google Keep / Apple Notes:

- Create a note per subject with the subject's color label
- Use it to jot down quick reminders during class when you can't open a planner
- Archive notes once tasks are done to keep things clean

Notion (for the more tech-savvy organizer):

- Set up a simple database with columns: Subject, Assignment, Due Date, Status
- Filter by subject or due date to see what's coming up
- Free and available on all devices

Physical Planner (still the gold standard for many people):

- Use colored pens or fine-tip markers to write each subject's assignments in that subject's color

- Check off or cross out tasks when complete—the physical satisfaction is real
- Flip to the week ahead every Sunday night

The Two-System Challenge

Not sure which system works for you? Try this:

- Pick two systems from above (example: physical binder + Google Calendar)
- Use BOTH for one week
- At the end of the week, journal: Which one did I actually use? Which one felt easier? Which one helped me miss less?
- Drop the one that felt like a chore. Keep the one that actually helped.

Glow Up Tracker Prompt: Which color helps you remember most? After one week of color-coding, write down which subject's assignments you stopped forgetting first. That's your most effective color pairing.

The Ultimate Homework Survival System—Never Forget an Assignment Again

Here's the number one reason students forget homework: They think they'll remember it later. They won't. Your brain is dealing with six classes, lunch drama, hallway chaos, and approximately forty-seven other things. "I'll remember it" is a lie your brain tells you.

The solution is simple: Write it down the second it's assigned. Not when you get home. Not during passing period. Right then.

> "I used to think I had a good memory. Then I started writing things down and realized how much I was missing. My grades went up a full letter in two subjects just from that one change."
>
> — Marcus, 6th grade

The Write-It-Down-Right-Away Mantra

Every time a teacher says any of the following, pick up your pen:

"For homework tonight…"

"This is due on…"

"Don't forget that…"

"Your test is on..."

"The project is due..."

"Make sure your parents sign..."

What to write:

Subject: Which class

Assignment: What exactly do you need to do

Due date: When it's due (be specific: "tomorrow" is not specific enough)

Materials needed: Anything you'll need that isn't already at home

If you missed it: *"Hey, could you repeat the due date? I want to make sure I have it right."* Teachers love this. It shows you care.

Backup move: Snap a photo of the board before you leave class. Do it every time without exception, especially for project instructions or multi-step assignments.

Breaking Down Big Projects: The Anti-Panic Method

The reason big projects feel overwhelming is that "write a five-page report" is not actually one task—it's about fifteen tasks. When you see it as one giant thing, your brain freezes. When you break it into small steps, it becomes manageable.

The Assignment Breakdown Template:

Assignment:

____

Total due date:

____

Steps to complete it:

Step 1: _____________________________ Mini-deadline: __________

Step 2: _____________________________ Mini-deadline: __________

Step 3: _____________________________ Mini-deadline: __________

Step 4: _____________________________ Mini-deadline: __________

Step 5: _____________________________ Mini-deadline: __________

· · ·

MATERIALS I NEED:

____

____

Who can I ask for help if I get stuck?

____

Example: "Write a five-paragraph essay on the water cycle" broken down:

Step 1: Review class notes and look up water cycle basics (15 min) — Monday

Step 2: Write an outline with main points for each paragraph — Monday

Step 3: Write the intro and first two body paragraphs — Tuesday

Step 4: Write the last body paragraph and conclusion — Wednesday

Step 5: Proofread, fix errors, format correctly — Thursday (due Friday)

See? Not one scary task. Five completely doable ones.

The Group Project Survival Plan

Group projects are their own special chaos. Here's how to keep them from becoming a disaster:

First meeting: Decide who does what IN WRITING. Take a photo of the task split.

Set group mini-deadlines: Each person's part is due two days before the final due date—so there's time to pull it together.

Create a group chat for the project only: Keep it separate from friend chats so nothing gets lost.

Check in midway: "Hey, where are we all at? I finished my part—does anyone need help?"

Have a backup plan: If someone drops the ball, who covers it? Having this conversation early prevents last-minute meltdowns.

Reminders and Accountability Beyond the Planner

Phone alarms:

Set an alarm for 4 PM every school day labeled "HW check—open planner."

Set alarms 2 days before any major due date, labeled with the specific assignment

Set a Sunday evening alarm labeled "Week ahead check—what's due this week?"

Sticky note wall:

Put sticky notes for upcoming deadlines on your bedroom mirror, desk, or door

Each note: subject + assignment + due date. Move them to a "done" section of your wall when complete

Seeing them every morning keeps your brain from forgetting

The accountability text:

"Hey, can you remind me to check my math homework tonight around 7?"

"Texting to remind you—science test tomorrow, study tonight!"

Find one friend who's also trying to get more organized. Check in on each other. It works.

The Late Night "Oh No" Checklist

You're about to go to bed when you realize you might have missed something. Don't panic. Run through this:

☐ Open planner/calendar. What's due tomorrow?

☐ Check your subject folders. Is anything in the "to turn in" pocket?

☐ Think through each class: math, English, science, social studies, electives. Anything?

☐ Check the class website or app if your school uses one—sometimes assignments are posted there

☐ Text a classmate: "Hey, quick question—was there anything due tomorrow in [subject]?"

☐ If there IS something and it's not done: How long will it actually take? Can you do it now? If not, see the next section.

The 20-minute rule: If something will take 20 minutes or less, just do it. The relief you'll feel going to bed with it done is worth way more than 20 minutes of sleep.

How to Crush Tests Without Cramming or Stressing

Cramming is when you study everything the night before a test, fueled by panic and probably too much sugar. It feels productive. It is not productive. Research is very clear that cramming leads to worse test performance than spreading studying out over multiple days, and you forget it all within 48 hours anyway.

The good news: Studying smarter doesn't mean studying more. It means studying differently. Here's how.

> "I used to cram the night before every test and wonder why I kept blanking out. My older sister showed me the two-week study plan thing, and I thought it was overkill. Then I tried it for a history test and got a B+ when I usually get Cs. Now I do it for everything."
>
> — Jordan, 7th grade

The Spaced Repetition Method (In Plain English)

Spaced repetition means reviewing material multiple times over several days instead of all at once. Here's a simple version:

Test in 5 days:

Day 1: Read notes, highlight key points, and make a brief outline

Day 2: Review your outline, try to recall it without looking, and fill in the gaps

Day 3: Quiz yourself (flashcards, practice questions, teach it out loud)

Day 4: Focus only on the stuff you got wrong on Day 3. Light review of the rest.

Day 5 (test day): Quick 10-minute review of your outline. You're ready.

Test in 2 weeks:

Days 1–2: Read notes, create a study guide or flashcards

Days 3–5: Review 10–15 minutes per day, quiz yourself

Days 6–8: Focus on weak spots, re-quiz

Days 9–11: Light review, confirm you still know the strong spots

Days 12–13: Final focused review of weak spots only

Day 14 (test day): 10-minute review, eat a good breakfast, you've got this

STUDY HACKS for Different Learning Styles

If you're a VISUAL learner (you think in pictures and diagrams):

- Color-code your notes by topic or importance
- Draw concept maps that show how ideas connect
- Turn lists into charts or timelines
- Use different colored highlighters for different categories of information
- Watch a short video on the topic (YouTube is genuinely helpful for this)

If you're an AUDITORY learner (you learn by hearing and talking):

- Read your notes OUT LOUD instead of silently
- Record yourself explaining the material and play it back
- Study with a friend and quiz each other verbally
- Make up a song, rap, or rhythm for things you need to memorize
- Explain the concept to a family member, as they've never heard of it

If you're a KINESTHETIC learner (you learn by doing):

- Write and rewrite key facts by hand (the physical act of writing locks it in)
- Make flashcards and physically sort them into "know it" and "need to review" piles
- Walk around while reviewing—seriously, movement helps retention
- Act out or physically represent the material if possible (great for history or science)
- Use apps like Quizlet that make studying interactive

The "Teach It" Method (works for everyone):

Explain the material out loud as if you're teaching it to someone who knows nothing about it. Use simple words. If you get stuck, that's the part you need to study more. If you can explain it clearly, you know it.

> "I explain things to my dog. He doesn't understand, but I do, so it works."
>
> — Tyler, 8th grade

Flashcard Challenge: Making Cards That Actually Work

Bad flashcards: Just copying the textbook definition on the back.

Good flashcards:

Front: A specific question, not just a term. Example: "What is the process called when water turns from liquid to gas?" (not just "Evaporation")

Back: The answer IN YOUR OWN WORDS, plus one example or image if helpful

Color: Use your subject color for the card border or a dot in the corner

App option: Quizlet lets you make digital flashcard sets, shuffle them, and test yourself—plus you can share sets with classmates

Pre-Test Calm-Down Routine

Feeling nervous before a test is normal. Your body is gearing up. But too much anxiety can actually block your ability to think clearly. Here's a quick routine to reset:

1. The Brain Dump (5 minutes before the test): On a scrap of paper or the back of scratch paper, write down every formula, date, name, or fact you're afraid you'll forget. Get it OUT of your head and onto paper. Now you don't have to hold it all in there.

2. Box Breathing (2 minutes): Breathe in for 4 counts. Hold for 4 counts. Breathe out for 4 counts. Hold for 4 counts. Repeat three times. This genuinely slows your heart rate.

3. The Power Phrase: Pick one sentence you tell yourself before every test. *"I've studied this, and I'm ready." "I know more than I think I do." "I can figure out what I don't immediately know."* Say it. Mean it.

4. Sharpen your focus: Before you start, quickly skim the whole test. See how many questions there are, notice the ones that look easiest, and go there first. This builds momentum.

Test-Day Survival Scripts

If you blank on a question:

"Circle it, move on, come back." Spending five minutes frozen on one question wastes time you could use on everything else. Mark it, move forward, return at the end.

If you need clarification from the teacher:

- *"Can you clarify what this question is asking?"*
- *"Is this asking about [X] or [Y]?"*
- *"Can I have a moment to re-read this question?"*

If you finish early:

Don't hand it in immediately. Use every remaining minute to:

• Re-read each question to make sure you answered what was actually asked

• Check math work by working backward

• Add detail to any short-answer questions that feel thin

• Change answers only if you have a clear reason—first instincts are usually right

How to Talk to Teachers About Late or Missing Work

"I Forgot My Worksheet!"—What to Say to Teachers (with Email Scripts)

It happens to everyone. Even the most organized people in the world sometimes forget things. What separates the students who handle it well from the ones who spiral is this: owning it quickly, calmly, and with a plan.

Teachers are human. They've forgotten things, too. Most of them are not sitting around hoping you fail—they want you to succeed. What they don't like is excuses, avoidance, or the classic "the dog ate it." What they DO respect is honesty, responsibility, and a student who takes initiative to fix the situation.

> "I forgot a big assignment once and spent two days not saying anything because I was embarrassed. By the time I told my teacher, it was worse. She said if I had just come to her on day one, she would've given me a day extension. I learned my lesson the hard way."
>
> — Amara, 6th grade

The In-Person Script: What to Actually Say

For a forgotten worksheet or simple assignment:

"I'm really sorry—I left my worksheet at home this morning. Is there any way I can bring it in tomorrow? I did complete it, it's just not with me."

For an assignment you genuinely didn't finish:

"I didn't finish [assignment], and I take responsibility for that. I'm not going to make excuses. Is there any possibility of turning it in late for partial credit? I want to make it right."

FOR A PROJECT, you need more time on:

"I want to be honest with you — I underestimated how long this project would take, and I'm not happy with where it is right now. Can I have until [specific date] to turn in something I'm actually proud of?"

What NOT to say:

• *"My printer broke."* (Unless it literally did — and even then, "I could have emailed it" is the follow-up teachers think.)

• *"My mom forgot to remind me."* (Your homework is your responsibility, not your mom's.)

• *"I didn't know it was due today."* (It was on the board. Own it.)

• *"It's not fair because…"* (This almost never helps.)

Tips for the conversation:

• Choose a good moment — before class, after class, or during a transition — not during a lecture

• Keep it brief. State the problem, take responsibility, make a request, say thank you

• Look them in the eye. It shows you're serious

• Accept whatever answer you get without arguing

The Email Script: When Talking In Person Feels Too Hard

Sometimes you're too nervous to have the conversation face-to-face, or a teacher isn't available before class. Email is a totally legitimate option. Here's how to write one that gets results:

Step-by-step email format:

1. **Subject line:** Clear and specific. "Question about [assignment name]" or "Missed Assignment — [Your Name], Period [X]"

2. **Greeting:** "Hi Mr./Ms. [Last Name]," — Always use their title and last name unless they've told you otherwise

3. **Body:** What happened + your responsibility + your request. Keep it to 3–4 sentences.

4. **Closing:** "Thank you for your time" or "I appreciate your understanding" + your name and class period

SAMPLE EMAIL:

Subject: Missing Assignment — Jordan Lee, Period 3

Hi Ms. Johnson, I wanted to reach out because I left my science worksheet at home today. I completed the assignment — it just isn't with me. Would it be possible to bring it in tomorrow for full or partial credit? I'm sorry for the inconvenience and will make sure to double-check my bag from now on. Thank you for your understanding. Jordan Lee, Period 3

Checklist before you hit send:

☐ Did I use their correct name and title?

☐ Did I take responsibility without making excuses?

☐ Did I make a specific, reasonable request?

☐ Did I thank them?

☐ Did I spell-check? (No ALL CAPS, no "hu" or "lol", no texting abbreviations)

☐ Did I include my name AND class period?

Building a Trustworthy Reputation with Teachers

Here's something most students don't realize: Teachers remember. Not in a creepy way — in a human way. They notice which students communicate when something goes wrong versus which ones just disappear. They notice who comes to them proactively versus who only shows up when they're failing. And that reputation affects how much grace they extend when you need it.

You don't have to be the teacher's pet. You just have to be a trustworthy student. Here's what that looks like:

☑ Turn things in on time consistently (even if they're not perfect)

☑ When you can't, communicate BEFORE the deadline, not after

☑ Follow through when you say you'll do something

☑ Say thank you when a teacher helps you out

☑ Show effort, even on hard assignments

Challenge: Zero forgotten assignments for one full week. Track your streak in your Glow Up Tracker. How does it feel at the end of the week to have turned in everything on time?

The "Brain Full" Problem—What to Do When It's All Too Much

Sometimes you sit down to do homework and your brain just… won't. You're staring at the page, you've read the same sentence four times, and you can feel yourself getting more stressed by the second because you're not doing it.

This isn't laziness. This is an overload. And it has a solution.

The Homework Triage Method

Triage is a medical term for sorting things by urgency. Apply it to homework:

⚠️ **URGENT (do tonight):**

- Due tomorrow

- Test to study for tomorrow

- Anything you've already pushed back once

⏰ **IMPORTANT (do in the next 1–2 days):**

- Due this week

- Multi-day projects you need to chip away at

- Study material for a test that's not tomorrow but is soon

✅ **CAN WAIT (later this week):**

- Due next week

- Optional or extra credit

- Reading for enrichment

Do Urgent first. Always. Then Important. Can Wait gets done when the other two are handled.

The Pomodoro Technique: Work Smarter in Chunks

Working for three hours straight without breaks is actually less productive than working in shorter, focused bursts. Here's a method that works:

1. **Set a timer for 25 minutes.** Work on ONE task. Phone face down, notifications off.

2. **When the timer goes off, stop.** Take a 5-minute break. Stretch, get water, breathe.

3. **Repeat.** After four 25-minute sessions, take a longer break (15–20 minutes).

Why it works: Your brain gets rest without losing momentum. The timer creates urgency. The endpoint is always visible, so it feels manageable.

App options: Forest, Be Focused, or just your phone's built-in timer.

Your Ideal Homework Environment

Not all spaces are equal for getting work done. Here's what actually matters:

- **Consistent spot:** Same desk, table, or corner every day. Your brain starts to associate that spot with focus.
- **Minimal distractions:** Phone in another room or on Do Not Disturb. TV off. Noisy siblings? Library, bedroom with door closed, or noise-canceling headphones.
- **Good lighting:** Natural light is best. If not, a lamp that doesn't strain your eyes.
- **Supplies ready:** Don't start working, then spend 10 minutes finding a pencil. Everything you need should be in front of you before you begin.
- **Optional: music:** Some people focus better with background music. Instrumentals or lo-fi beats tend to work better than songs with lyrics. Experiment and see what works for you.

> "I started doing homework at the library instead of my bedroom, and everything changed. At home, I always found a reason to stop. At the library, there was nothing else to do but work."
>
> — Destiny, 7th grade

Organization Glow Up Tracker

Organization isn't built overnight. It's built through small habits practiced consistently. Use this tracker to notice what's working, what isn't, and where you're getting better.

Week of:

ASSIGNMENT TRACKING:

Did I write down every assignment this week as it was assigned?

Mon ☐ Tue ☐ Wed ☐ Thu ☐ Fri ☐

TURNED IN ON TIME:

Check each assignment you turned in on time this week:

____

ANYTHING LATE OR MISSING:

If so, what happened and what will you do differently?

____

____

STUDY SYSTEM CHECK:

Did I study in advance for any tests this week (not just the night before)?

☐ Yes — What worked?

____

☐ No — What got in the way?

____

MY ORGANIZATION WIN THIS WEEK:

(Even small: found a missing paper, remembered a deadline, sent an email to a teacher, etc.)

____

____

ORGANIZATION CONFIDENCE CHECK:

How in control of my schoolwork do I feel this week?

1 --------- 2 --------- 3 --------- 4 --------- 5 --------- 6 --------- 7 --------- 8 --------- 9 --------- 10

ONE SYSTEM I WANT TO TRY NEXT WEEK:

____

Monthly Reflection

• Which color-coding or organizational system am I actually using consistently?

• What's the assignment or deadline I'm most proud of not forgetting?

• When did I study in advance and notice a difference?

• What's one organizational habit that has actually become automatic?

• What's still feeling chaotic that I want to tackle next month?

You've Got This—For Real

Here's what you now know how to do:

• Set up a color-code system that makes your binder and calendar actually make sense

• Write down every assignment the second it's given so nothing slips through the cracks

• Break big projects into small, doable steps with mini-deadlines

• Study smarter by spreading it out instead of cramming

• Use a pre-test routine to calm your nerves and sharpen your focus

• Handle a forgotten assignment with an honest conversation or a well-written email

• Triage your homework so the most urgent things get done first

• Create an environment where your brain can actually focus

Organization isn't about being perfect. It's about having systems that catch you when your memory fails, which it will—because you're a middle schooler with a million things going on, not a robot. Build the systems. Trust the systems. Let them do the remembering for you.

confidence boosters for awkward moments

Here's something nobody tells you about confidence: It's not a feeling. It's a skill. Confident people don't walk through middle school immune to embarrassment or awkwardness. They just get really good at recovering. They know how to shake something off, laugh at themselves, reset after a stumble, and keep moving—without the moment defining the rest of their day.

The awkward moments? Those aren't going away. Voice cracks mid-presentation. Lunches fall off trays. Brilliant answers come out totally backwards. Someone calls you out in front of the whole class at exactly the wrong time. This is middle school. It's part of the deal.

This chapter will give you a recovery toolkit. Because the goal isn't to have awkward moments—it's to get so good at bouncing back that the moments stop feeling like catastrophes and start feeling like… stories you'll tell later.

> "I tripped walking up to receive an award at the eighth-grade ceremony. In front of the entire school and all the parents. I laughed, took a bow, and kept walking. Everyone clapped. It became my whole personality for a week. Now it's just a great story."
>
> — Zoe, 9th grade

Laughing Off Locker Disasters (and Other Epic Fails)

Let's start with the classics. The moments that feel massive in the second they happen, but are almost always forgotten by the next day. Lockers jam. Stuff spills. You walk into a door that you thought was open. You call your teacher "Mom." These things happen to everyone—and the way you handle them in the moment is everything.

The Hall of Fame of Middle School Fails

Real middle schoolers, real moments:

> "I opened my locker too fast, and everything fell out. Like, everything. My binder exploded. Papers everywhere. I just stood there staring at the pile on the floor while people walked around it. Finally, I said, 'Well, this is my life now,' and started picking it up. A kid I'd never talked to stopped and helped me. We became friends."

> — Noah, 7th grade

> "I was raising my hand to answer a question, and I accidentally knocked my water bottle off the desk. It hit the floor, the lid flew off, and water went everywhere, including on the kid next to me. I wanted to evaporate. My teacher just handed me paper towels and said, 'it happens to the best of us.'"

> — Lily, 6th grade

> "I called my science teacher 'Dad' once. Out loud. In front of everyone. He paused and said, 'I'm flattered.' The class lost it. I turned so red. But honestly? Everyone forgot about it by the next class."

> — Ethan, 6th grade

Notice anything? In every single one of these stories, the world did not end. Nobody transferred schools. Life continued. And in most cases, the moment became something that brought people together rather than pushing them apart.

The trick? How you respond in the three seconds after it happens.

The Three-Second Recovery Rule

You have about three seconds after an awkward moment, where the whole room is watching to see what you do next. Your response in those three seconds determines whether the moment becomes a big deal or a blip.

The Three-Second Recovery Formula:

1. Breathe. One quick breath. Not dramatic. Just a reset.

2. React visibly. Smile, laugh, shake your head. Something that says "I see what just happened." Pretending nothing happened when clearly something did makes it MORE awkward.

3. Say or do something light. One quick phrase to break the tension, then move on. Done.

The Locker Disaster Rescue Kit: Scripts for Every Fail

Your locker explodes / everything falls out:

"And the locker wins again." [Smile, start picking it up]

"Well, I needed to clean this out anyway."

"Nothing to see here, totally intentional."

You trip in the hallway:

"Floor: 1. Me: 0."

"That's called a controlled fall."

"I'm good! Gravity and I are just very close."

You walk into the wrong classroom (again):

"Oops—touring the building. Carry on."

"Wrong room, right building. Progress."

You call the teacher the wrong name / call them Mom or Dad:

"I'm so sorry—I promise I know your name." [Laugh it off]

"That came out wrong. I meant [correct name]."

You drop your lunch tray:

"Absolutely nailed that."

"And I'm accepting zero notes on my performance."

"Is there a way to make this look intentional? No? Okay."

You say something in class, and it comes out completely backwards:

"Let me try that again with actual words."

"My brain and my mouth are not on speaking terms today."

WHY SELF-DEPRECATING HUMOR Works (And When It Doesn't)

Self-deprecating humor—making a light joke at your own expense—is one of the most powerful social tools you have. When you laugh at yourself first, you take away the power of anyone else laughing at you. You're in on the joke. You're confident enough not to take yourself too seriously. That's magnetic.

It works when:

✔ The situation is genuinely funny or harmless

✔ You keep it light and brief—one joke, then move on

✔ You're laughing with the situation, not beating yourself up

✔ Your tone says "I'm fine, this is funny," not "I'm a disaster."

It doesn't work when:

⚠ You turn one joke into a whole apology tour—one line is enough

⚠ Your humor is actually self-criticism in disguise ("I'm so stupid" dressed up as a joke)

⚠ The situation is actually serious, and humor feels dismissive

⚠ You're using it to mask real distress—if something genuinely hurts, you don't have to pretend it's funny

The line: Laughing at a specific moment is healthy. Laughing at yourself as a person is not. "That fall was hilarious" is very different from "I'm such an idiot." Know the difference.

The Fail-to-Story Pipeline

Here's a reframe that changes everything: Your most embarrassing moments are your best future stories. The moments people love to hear aren't the polished, perfect ones—they're the ones where something went hilariously wrong, and you survived.

Glow Up Tracker Prompt: Write down your funniest fail this week. What happened? How did you handle it? What would you do the same way again? The act of writing it as a "story" instead of a "disaster" shifts how you feel about it.

Turning Awkward Presentations into Power Moves

Public speaking is consistently ranked as one of the top fears of humans of all ages—and middle schoolers are absolutely not exempt. Standing up in front of your class while your heart tries to exit your chest through your ribcage is a genuinely uncomfortable experience.

But here's what changes everything: Every single person sitting in those seats has either already gone through it or is dreading their own turn. They are not your enemies. They are your fellow survivors. And your teacher is on your side—they want you to succeed.

Let's talk about the most common presentation disasters and exactly how to handle each one.

The Most Common Presentation Fears (And the Truth About Each One)

Fear #1: "My voice is going to crack."

Truth: Voice cracks happen to everyone at this age. They are a biological fact of puberty, not a personal failure. If it happens, take a quick sip of water (always have water with you), pause for a breath, and keep going. Most audiences barely notice, and if they do, they're sympathetic—not cruel.

Fear #2: "I'm going to forget everything."

Truth: You won't forget everything. You might blank on one part. That's different. And there are specific strategies for this—see below.

Fear #3: "Everyone is going to laugh at me."

Truth: Most of your classmates are either paying half-attention, relieved it's not their turn, or genuinely rooting for you. The people who would laugh cruelly at a mistake are rare—and a teacher is right there.

Fear #4: "I'm going to trip walking up."

Truth: This occasionally happens. If it does, refer to the Three-Second Recovery Rule and the scripts above. A graceful recovery from a trip can actually make an audience like you more.

Fear #5: "I'll turn bright red, and everyone will notice."

Truth: Blushing is a physical response your body does automatically, and you cannot control it. Trying to hide it makes it worse. The fastest way to get past a blush is to acknowledge it lightly ("I can feel myself turning red—totally normal, moving on") and continue. Once you stop fighting it, it fades faster

Before You Go Up: The Power Prep Routine

In the minutes before your presentation, do this:

1. Review your opening line only. Not the whole thing—just how you start. If you can get through your first sentence confidently, momentum carries you forward.

2. The "smell the pizza, blow out the candles" breath. Breathe in slowly through your nose (like you're smelling something amazing). Breathe out slowly through your mouth (like you're blowing out birthday candles). Do this three times. It physically slows your heart rate.

3. Power pose for 30 seconds. Find a private spot—bathroom, hallway, empty corner. Stand with your feet shoulder-width apart, hands on your hips or raised above your head in a V shape. Hold for 30 seconds. Research suggests this genuinely affects how confident you feel.

4. Scan for a friendly face. Before you start, find one person in the audience who you know is on your side—a friend, someone who smiles at you. That's your anchor point.

During the Presentation: Confidence Hacks That Actually Work

Slow down.

When you're nervous, your brain speeds up, and so does your mouth. You'll feel like you're going too slow—you're not. Slow = clear, calm, and in control. Fast = hard to follow and sounds panicked.

Make eye contact with friendly faces first.

Don't scan the whole room randomly. Pick two or three friendly faces and rotate between them. This makes you look confident and engaged without the pressure of meeting every set of eyes.

Pause on purpose.

A deliberate pause between sections or after an important point looks like confidence. It gives the audience time to absorb what you said. It gives you a second to breathe and remember what comes next. Silence is not your enemy.

Use audience engagement as a reset.

If you lose your place or feel panicked, ask the class a question: "Does anyone want to guess what happens next?" or "Has anyone else experienced this?" It buys you 15–20 seconds to regroup while looking like an engaging presenter.

When It Goes Wrong Mid-Presentation: Recovery Scripts

You completely blank and forget what comes next:

"Let me just take a second to check my notes—bear with me."

"I had a great point here — give me just a moment."

Then glance at your notes or notecards. Nobody will think less of you. Everyone will be relieved you recovered calmly.

You say the wrong word or get your facts mixed up:

"Actually, let me correct that — what I meant to say was…"

"I misspoke — the correct information is…"

Correcting yourself shows awareness and confidence, not weakness.

Someone in the class laughs or makes a comment:

"I'll take that as audience participation." [Keep going]

"Moving on —" [Don't acknowledge it further]

The teacher will handle it. Your job is to keep going. Don't engage, don't freeze, don't look wounded. The fastest way to neutralize a rude comment is to not give it any energy.

You trip on the way up or knock something over:

"And we're starting with a little drama." [Smile, settle, begin]

"Great entrance. Anyway —"

After the Presentation: The Real Debrief

The moment you sit back down, your brain will want to replay every single thing that went wrong. Do not let it. Here's how to debrief like someone who's building a skill rather than judging a performance:

Glow Up Tracker Prompt — Presentation Edition:

My nervousness level before: ___ / 10

My nervousness level after: ___ / 10

One thing that went better than I expected:

One moment I want to handle differently next time:

One thing I'm proud of myself for doing:

Every presentation makes the next one easier. Not because you stop being nervous — but because you've survived it before, and your brain starts to remember that.

> "I bombed my first presentation in sixth grade. Like,
> read off the paper the entire time, barely looked up,
> everyone could see the paper shaking. By eighth
> grade, I was chosen to present at the school board
> meeting. It only got better because I kept doing it."
> — Isaiah, 9th grade

What to Do When You Get Called Out (and Everyone's Watching)

Getting called out—whether by a teacher for not paying attention, by a peer for saying something wrong, or just being put on the spot at the worst possible moment—triggers a very specific kind of panic. Your face gets hot. Your mind goes blank. You feel like every pair of eyes in the room is a spotlight pointed directly at you.

Here's what you need to know: This feeling lasts about ninety seconds. It feels permanent, but it isn't. And how you respond in those ninety seconds is totally in your control.

The Most Common "Called Out" Scenarios

Scenario 1: Teacher calls on you, and you weren't paying attention.

The honest play always wins here:

"Sorry—I zoned out for a second. Could you repeat the question?"

"My bad. Can I hear that again?"

Don't fake an answer. Don't pretend you heard something you didn't. Teachers can always tell, and a confident "I lost focus, can you repeat that" lands so much better than a wrong guess delivered with false confidence.

Scenario 2: You answer a question, and you're wrong.

"Ah—okay, that's not right. What's the actual answer?"

"Well, I learned something. Good to know."

"Good to know—I'll remember that now."

Being wrong is not a character flaw. It's how you find out what you don't know yet. The students who make the most progress in school are the ones who answer wrong out loud, get corrected, and file it away. The ones who never answer to avoid being wrong… stay stuck.

Scenario 3: A peer calls you out or challenges you in front of others.

This one's trickier because there's a social element—it might feel like they're trying to embarrass you or score points in front of the group. Here's how to handle it without escalating:

"Interesting point—I see it differently, but okay."

"That's fair. I might be wrong about that."

"Hmm. Worth thinking about."

These responses are disarming. They don't concede if you don't believe you're wrong, but they don't escalate either. You stay calm. You look unrattled. That's the win.

Scenario 4: You make a loud, obvious mistake (knock something over, say something weird, etc.) mid-class.

See Section 1's recovery scripts. Apply. Move on. The faster you move on, the faster everyone else does, too.

The Four-Step Reset: Getting Your Composure Back Fast

Whether you're called out or you just had a moment, use this four-step reset to come back to yourself:

1. **Pause.** One full second of silence before you respond. It feels longer to you than it looks to everyone else. This pause keeps you from saying something reactive.
2. **Breathe.** One quiet breath in. Let it out slowly. This is invisible to the room but sends a signal to your nervous system to calm down.
3. **Small smile or neutral expression.** Not a forced grin—just a relaxed face. It signals to your brain that the situation is manageable. It signals to the room that you're not shattered.
4. **Respond, then continue.** Use one of the scripts above, then keep moving. Don't linger on the moment longer than necessary.

The mantra: *"I can handle this. It's not a big deal. I've gotten through worse."* Say it in your head in the pause before you respond. Mean it.

After a Tough Public Moment: The Recovery Plan

Sometimes you need more than ninety seconds to recover. That's okay. Here's what to do after class:

• **Text someone who gets it.** Not to vent publicly—just to someone safe who'll say "that sounds rough, you handled it though."

• **Give it context.** Ask yourself honestly: Will this matter in a week? In a month? If the answer is no (and it usually is), give yourself permission to let it go.

• **Write it out.** Use your Glow Up Journal. Getting it out of your head and onto paper takes away some of its power.

• **Do something physical.** Walk, shoot hoops, dance, whatever. Physical movement genuinely helps process stress and embarrassment.

• **Talk to a trusted adult if needed.** If it was truly humiliating and affecting you more than a day later, loop in someone you trust. Not every hard moment has to be handled alone.

> "I gave a wrong answer in math, and someone snickered. I turned red, said 'yep, that's wrong, good to know' and kept looking at the teacher. My teacher moved on, and we all moved on. Later that same kid got something wrong, and I didn't snicker. That felt good, too."
>
> — Camille, 7th grade

Building Real Confidence—Not the Fake "Just Be Yourself!" Kind

You've probably heard "just be confident!" or "just be yourself!" approximately eight thousand times. And you've probably noticed that this advice tells you what to do but not how to do it. Let's fix that.

Real confidence doesn't come from never feeling scared or awkward. It comes from having evidence that you can handle hard things. Every time you recover from an awkward moment, every time you give a presentation and survive, every time you get called out and respond with grace—you're adding to a bank of proof. "I've done hard things before. I can do them again."

The Confidence Bank: Making Deposits

Every brave, uncomfortable, or challenging thing you do—even if it goes imperfectly—is a deposit in your confidence bank. Here are ways to make deposits:

• **Do one uncomfortable thing per week intentionally.** Answer a question in class when you're not totally sure. Say hi first. Try something new. It doesn't have to be huge. Small deposits add up.

• **Track your hard moments and survival rate.** Look back at your Glow Up Tracker. How many hard things have you survived? That's evidence. Real evidence that you handle things.

• **Stop waiting to "feel" confident before you act.** Action comes first. Confidence follows. Not the other way around. You don't feel confident, then try—you try, then feel confident.

• **Notice what you do well.** Not to brag. Just to notice. You probably have more going for you than your inner critic is willing to admit.

The Inner Critic vs. The Inner Coach

Everyone has an inner critic—that voice in your head that narrates every mistake and worst-case scenario. Left unchecked, it runs the show. Here's how to turn the volume down on the critic and turn up the coach:

When the inner critic says... the inner coach responds:

- *"You sounded so stupid."* → *"You tried. That took courage. Next time will be smoother."*
- *"Everyone was judging you."* → *"Most people were thinking about themselves. This moment is smaller than it feels."*
- *"You'll never be good at this."* → *"You're getting better every time you do it. That's how it works."*
- *"That was humiliating."* → *"That was uncomfortable. Uncomfortable and humiliating are not the same thing."*
- *"Why do you even try?"* → *"Because trying is how you get better. That's the whole point."*

Practice: Next time your inner critic fires up, literally say "coach?" in your head and let the coach answer. It sounds weird. It works.

Confidence in Your Body Before Your Brain Catches Up

Your body and your brain communicate constantly. If your body is hunched, closed off, and making itself small, your brain gets the message that you're not safe. If your body is upright, open, and taking up its rightful space, your brain gets a different message entirely.

You can fake it physically even when you don't feel it yet:

1. **Walk like you know where you're going.** Even if you don't. Purposeful walking signals confidence to everyone around you— and to your own brain.

2. **Take up your space.** Don't shrink into corners or make yourself small. Sit fully in your chair. Stand with your feet planted. You have a right to be here.
3. **Speak at a volume people can hear.** Quiet voices signal insecurity. You don't have to be loud—just audible. Project slightly more than you think you need to.
4. **Uncross your arms.** Crossed arms are protective but they also signal to others (and to you) that you're closed off. Let your arms relax.
5. **Make eye contact.** Not staring—just steady, comfortable eye contact during conversations. It signals that you're present and that you respect the person you're talking to.

The "Glow Up" Journal—How to See Your Progress, One Awkward Moment at a Time

You've seen Glow Up Tracker prompts throughout this book. This section is about going deeper: building a full Glow Up Journal practice that helps you actually see—in writing, in your own words—how much you're growing.

Here's why this matters: Your brain is wired to notice problems and threats. It's very good at cataloging what went wrong and not nearly as good at registering what went right. The journal is how you correct for that. It's how you see yourself more accurately.

What the Glow Up Journal Is (And Isn't)

It IS:

☑ A record of your growth, including the messy parts

☑ A place to process awkward moments as stories, not disasters

☑ Evidence you can look back on when you forget how far you've come

☑ Completely private—for your eyes only unless you choose to share

☑ Flexible—words, doodles, bullet points, whatever works for you

It IS NOT:

🚫 A highlight reel of only perfect moments

🚫 A place to beat yourself up

🚫 A chore—if it feels like homework, you're doing it wrong

🚫 Required to be neat, polished, or grammatically correct

THE CORE ENTRY Template

Use this format for any entry—a tough moment, a win, a weird day, or just a reflection:

GLOW UP JOURNAL ENTRY

Date: _________________

Mood right now (emoji or word): _________________________________

What happened:

(Describe the moment—funny, hard, embarrassing, or good. Be specific.)

____

____

____

How I felt in the moment:

____

____

What I did:

(How did you respond? What script or strategy did you use, even if imperfectly?)

____

____

What I'd do the same next time:

____

What I'd try differently:

____

One thing I'm proud of from this moment (even something tiny):

____

Bonus doodle space: Draw your mood, your face in the moment, or just scribble. It counts.

THE MONTHLY GLOW Up Review

Once a month, flip back through your entries and answer these:

• What was my funniest fail? How did I handle it?

• What's one moment where I surprised myself?

• What's one situation I handled better this month than I would have three months ago?

• What's my most creative recovery?

• What do I want to work on next month?

• On a scale of 1–10, how has my confidence in bouncing back shifted since I started this journal?

The Glow Up Show & Tell (Optional But Powerful)

At some point, consider sharing one entry—just one—with someone you trust completely. A best friend. A parent. A counselor. A sibling.

Not because you have to. But because sharing a story of something hard you got through, out loud with someone who cares about you, makes it more real. It turns a private win into a witnessed one. And witnessed wins stick.

> "I showed my mom one of my journal entries about bombing a presentation, and she told me about the time she forgot her entire speech at a work conference and had to improvise. I had no idea. It made me feel so much less alone."
>
> — Gabrielle, 7th grade

Sample Entry: So You Know What This Looks Like

Date: November 4 2026 **Mood:** 😬 → 😌

What happened: I was giving my history presentation and completely blanked on my third point. Like, full blackout. I stood there for what felt like ten years. I finally said, "Let me check my notes for this part," and looked at my notecard. Found it. Kept going. The teacher smiled at me.

How I felt in the moment: Like I wanted the floor to open up. Total panic.

What I did: Used the "let me check my notes" script. Took a breath. Kept going.

What I'd do the same: The script. It worked. People barely noticed.

What I'd try differently: Practice out loud more so I know it better. I practiced in my head, but that's different.

One thing I'm proud of: I didn't run out of the room. I kept going. That's huge for me.

You're Already Braver Than You Think

Let's recap what you now have in your confidence toolkit:

- The three-second recovery rule for any awkward moment
- Scripts for every classic middle school fail—lockers, trips, wrong classrooms, and all
- A full presentation prep and recovery system
- Scripts for every version of being called out—by teachers, by peers, by the universe
- The four-step reset to get your composure back fast
- The confidence bank concept—why doing hard things builds the real thing
- The inner critic vs. inner coach framework
- Body language basics that signal confidence before you feel it
- A Glow Up Journal system for tracking your growth, one awkward moment at a time

Confidence isn't a personality type you either have or don't. It's a collection of small moments where you tried something hard, handled something awkward, or kept going when your instinct was to hide. You're building it every single day—even on the days it doesn't feel like it.

big feelings, real solutions— managing stress, anxiety, and mood swings

Middle school feelings are not small feelings. They are enormous, sudden, confusing, and sometimes completely out of proportion to whatever just happened. One minute you're fine; the next you're upset about something you can't even fully explain. You feel stressed about a test, then stressed about being stressed. You're excited about something on Monday and can't remember why you cared by Wednesday.

If this sounds familiar, here's what you need to know: This is not you being "too sensitive" or "dramatic." This is you having a human brain in the middle of one of the most intense developmental periods of your entire life. The emotional rollercoaster is real, it's biological, and it happens to everyone.

This chapter is about understanding what's happening, building a toolkit for the hard moments, and knowing when and how to ask for help. Because big feelings deserve real solutions—not just "just calm down" or "stop worrying about it."

"Is This Normal?"—Understanding Stress and Mood Swings

Let's start with the big question many middle schoolers wonder but don't always ask out loud: Is what I'm feeling normal?

The answer, almost always, is YES. Here's why.

What's Actually Happening in Your Brain Right Now

Your brain is undergoing more change right now than it will at any other point in your life except infancy. The prefrontal cortex—the part that handles decision-making, emotional regulation, and impulse control—is under major construction and won't be fully developed until your mid-twenties. Meanwhile, the emotional center of your brain (the amygdala) is working overtime.

Translation: Your emotions are running on a high-powered engine, and the brakes are still being installed. That's why feelings can come on fast, feel huge, and take longer to settle than you'd like.

Add to that: hormones shifting, a more complex social world than you've ever navigated, higher academic expectations, and a phone that delivers a constant stream of information and social feedback. It's a lot. Of course, it's a lot.

The Mood Meter: What's Common and What to Notice

Totally normal middle school feelings:

☑ **Stress:** Feeling overwhelmed by too much to do, too many expectations, or uncertain outcomes

☑ **Anxiety:** Worry about things that might happen, social situations, tests, or just a general sense of dread you can't quite name

☑ **Irritability:** Snapping at people for small things, low tolerance for frustration, feeling prickly

☑ **Sadness:** Low moods that come and go, sometimes without a clear reason

☑ **Loneliness:** Even when surrounded by people, one sometimes feeling unseen or disconnected

☑ **Mood swings:** Fine one hour, upset the next, fine again by dinner

☑ **Emotional intensity:** Feeling things much more strongly than they seem to warrant

Signs it might be more than typical stress (worth talking to a trusted adult about):

! Feelings of sadness or emptiness that last more than two weeks

! Anxiety that makes it hard to go to school, eat, sleep, or be around people

! Losing interest in things you used to enjoy

! Feeling hopeless, worthless, or like things will never get better

! Physical symptoms with no medical cause (stomachaches, headaches every day)

! Thoughts of hurting yourself

Note: This list isn't meant to scare you. Most middle schoolers experience the first list and not the second. But if you recognize things in the second list, please talk to an adult you trust. You deserve support—and help is available.

Real Middle Schoolers on What "Normal" Feels Like

"I used to cry about tests and then feel embarrassed about crying about tests, which made me cry more. My counselor told me that was just my brain taking school seriously. Now I just let myself feel it for a few minutes and then do something about it."

— Priya, 7th grade

"Some days I want to hang out with everyone. Other days I want to be completely alone, and I don't know why. My mom thinks something's wrong when I go quiet but I'm just recharging. That's a thing people can do."

— Marcus, 8th grade

"I get stressed about things that haven't happened yet. Like, I'll stress about a test two weeks away. My older sister says she still does that. At least I know it's not just me."

— Aisha, 6th grade

Stress Triggers: What Sets You Off?

Knowing your personal stress triggers is one of the most useful things you can do. Different people stress about different things. Common middle school triggers:

✓ Academic pressure (grades, tests, assignments piling up)

✓ Social situations (fitting in, friend drama, feeling left out)

✓ Performance anxiety (presentations, sports, auditions, tryouts)

✓ Family stress (arguments at home, changes in family structure, parents' stress)

✓ Too many commitments (school + sports + clubs + social life + homework = overload)

✓ Uncertainty (not knowing what's going to happen, big transitions)

✓ Comparison (feeling behind other people, scrolling through other people's lives)

✓ Physical changes (body image, puberty, feeling uncomfortable in your own skin)

Glow Up Tracker Prompt: List three things that stress you out most and three things that reliably help your mood. Knowing both sides of this equation is power.

Your Personal Mood Tracker

Track your mood daily for two weeks. At the end of each day, rate your overall mood and note what might have affected it:

Daily Mood Tracker

Rate 1–10 (1 = rough day, 10 = great day). Note one thing that affected your mood.

Mon: ___ / 10　What happened: _______________________________________

Tue: ___ / 10　What happened: _______________________________________

Wed: ___ / 10　What happened: _______________________________________

Thu: ___ / 10　What happened: _______________________________________

Fri: ___ / 10　What happened: _______________________________________

Sat: ___ / 10　What happened: _______________________________________

Sun: ___ / 10　What happened: _______________________________________

After two weeks, look for patterns. Which days are consistently harder? Which situations tank your mood? Which ones lift it? That's your data.

Mindfulness Hacks That Don't Feel Cringe

When most people hear "mindfulness," they picture someone sitting cross-legged on a cushion, humming with their eyes closed. And maybe that's your thing—in which case, great. But for most middle schoolers, that image is enough to make them close the book.

So let's rebrand. Mindfulness is not meditation. It's not spiritual. It's not something you have to be good at or do perfectly. It's just the practice of paying attention to what's happening right now instead of spinning out about what happened earlier or what might happen next. And it turns out your brain really needs this, especially when it's in overdrive.

Here are practical, non-awkward ways to do it.

Mini-Mindfulness: 30-Second Resets

These take less than a minute and can be done anywhere—at your desk, in the hallway, in the bathroom, at lunch:

THE 5-4-3-2-1 GROUNDING Exercise

When your thoughts are spiraling, this pulls you back into the present moment:

5 things you can SEE: Look around. Name them in your head. The ceiling tile. Your pencil. Someone's jacket. The window. The clock.

4 things you can TOUCH: Your feet on the floor. The texture of your desk. The weight of your backpack strap. The fabric of your shirt.

3 things you can HEAR: The hum of the air vent. Someone's pencil scratching. A door is closing down the hall.

2 things you can SMELL: Even subtle smells count. Lunch from the cafeteria. Your own shampoo.

1 thing you can TASTE: The water you just drank. Lingering lunch. Gum if you have it.

By the time you finish, you've been fully in your body for about 60 seconds instead of in your head. The anxiety doesn't always disappear, but it gets smaller.

The Anchor Breath

One breath, done intentionally. Breathe in slowly through your nose for four counts. Hold for two. Out through your mouth for six. That's it. Just one. Your nervous system responds to this faster than you'd expect.

The Name-It Move

When you're feeling something intense, name it out loud or in your head: "I'm anxious right now." "I'm frustrated." "I feel really overwhelmed." Research shows that labeling an emotion reduces its intensity by activating the rational part of your brain. You're not suppressing the feeling—you're just getting out of the driver's seat and into the passenger seat for a second.

The Fidget Focus

Keep something small in your pocket—a smooth stone, a small fidget ring, a textured eraser. When you feel anxiety rising, hold it and focus on the physical sensation. Temperature. Texture. Weight. This grounds you in the present without anyone around you even knowing.

Everyday Mindful Moments (No Cushion Required)

You don't have to create a special time for mindfulness. You can slip it into things you're already doing:

• **Mindful walking:** On your way between classes, notice the feeling of your feet hitting the floor. The sounds around you. The temperature of the air. Just for one hallway. That's it.

• **Mindful eating:** At lunch, eat the first few bites of something slowly and actually notice what it tastes like. You're not doing anything extra—just paying attention to what you're already doing.

• **Mindful doodling:** If you doodle during class (we all know it happens), do it with full attention. Notice the shapes you make. The pressure of the pen. This is actually a legitimate mindfulness practice.

• **Mindful music:** Pick one song and listen to it on the way home from school with your full attention—not as background noise, but actually listening. Notice the instruments. The lyrics. The shifts in tempo. One song, full attention.

• **The morning pause:** Before you get out of bed, take ten seconds to just notice how you feel. Not to judge it or fix it. Just to notice. This builds self-awareness over time.

Invent Your Own Hack

The best mindfulness practice is the one you'll actually use. Here's your space to brainstorm:

A moment in my day when I feel most anxious or stressed:

____

Something small I could do in that moment to pause and reset:

____

What I want to call my hack (give it a name you'll remember):

____

Challenge: Try your hack once a day for one week. After seven days, write in your Glow Up Journal: Did it help? What would you tweak? What will you keep?

Panic Button: Quick Calming Tricks for Tests, Presentations, and Drama

Sometimes you need more than a mindful breath. Sometimes you're sitting at your desk, and your heart is racing, your hands are sweaty, you can't think straight, and you have to take a test in four minutes. That's not a mindfulness moment—that's a panic moment. And it needs a different kind of tool.

Know Your Warning Signs

Panic and overwhelm give you signals before they peak. Learn yours so you can catch it early:

Body signals:

- Heart racing or pounding

- Shallow or fast breathing

- Sweaty palms or shaky hands

- Tight chest or stomach

- Feeling hot or flushed

- Nausea or that "sick" feeling

- Tunnel vision or feeling dizzy

Mind signals:

- Thoughts racing or repeating in a loop

- "I can't do this" or "I'm going to fail" thoughts

- Inability to focus or follow a train of thought

- Catastrophizing ("This will ruin everything")

- Feeling detached, like you're watching yourself from the outside

The earlier you catch these signals, the faster you can intervene. Don't wait until you're in full panic mode.

The Panic Plan: Situation by Situation

TEST ANXIETY: You're sitting down, and your mind goes blank.

1. **Feet flat on the floor.** Literally press your feet into the ground. This physical grounding does something real.
2. **Box breathing:** In for 4, hold for 4, out for 4, hold for 4. Do this twice. Your heart rate will slow.
3. **Brain dump:** On the corner of your scratch paper, write down everything you're afraid you'll forget. Get it out of your head.
4. **Start with what you know:** Scan the test. Go to any question you can answer confidently. Build momentum before tackling the hard ones.
5. **Self-talk:** *"I've studied this. I know more than I think. I can figure out what I don't immediately know."*

PRESENTATION NERVES: You're about to go up, and you're shaking.

1. **The anchor object:** Hold something small in your non-dominant hand (a smooth stone, a folded piece of paper, a ring). Focus on the physical sensation for ten seconds.
2. **Feet and floor:** Feel the floor under your feet. You are physically stable. Your body can do this even when your mind is freaking out.
3. **Your opening line only:** Don't try to mentally rehearse the whole thing. Just your first sentence. If you can get that out, the rest follows.
4. **Silent mantra:** *"I've prepared for this. I know this material. The room is on my side."*

SOCIAL DRAMA: You just found out something upsetting, and you're about to walk into class.

1. **Give yourself permission to feel it later.** You don't have to process it right now. You can put it in a mental "box" with a note that says, "I'll deal with this after school." This is not suppression—it's strategic delay.
2. **Name it:** *"I'm upset right now, and that's okay. I don't have to fix it in the next four minutes."*
3. **Text a safe person:** "Hey, something happened. Can we talk after school?" Knowing help is waiting makes the next few hours more manageable.
4. **Focus on one thing at a time:** Just this class. Just this hour. Not the whole day, not the whole situation. Just right now.

Invisible Calm Tricks for When You Can't Be Obvious About It

Sometimes you're in the middle of class, and you need to calm down without anyone knowing. Here are techniques that are completely invisible:

Thumb-and-finger press: Press your thumb and pointer finger together firmly and hold for ten seconds. The pressure is grounding, and no one can see it.

Desk tap code: Tap a slow, quiet rhythm on your leg or the underside of your desk. The rhythmic repetition is calming.

Foot press: Press both feet firmly into the floor and focus on the sensation for thirty seconds. Invisible, effective.

Slow blink: Blink your eyes slowly, like a cat. It's the least conspicuous breathing exercise that exists.

Cold water (if available): If you can get to a water fountain or bathroom, splash cold water on your wrists. The temperature change activates your body's calming response.

> "I used to get so anxious during tests that I'd use the first ten minutes just trying to calm down. My counselor taught me the brain dump and the box breathing thing. Now I do both before the test even gets handed out. It changed everything."
>
> — Devon, 7th grade

When You're Overwhelmed: Who to Talk To, What to Say, and When to Hit Pause

There's a difference between stress you can manage on your own and stress that needs support. Both are valid. Neither one means you're weak. But knowing the difference — and knowing how to reach out when you need to — is one of the most important life skills you can build.

Signs You Need More Than a Self-Help Tool

You've tried the breathing exercises. You've journaled. You've talked to a friend. And it's still not better. Or it keeps coming back. Or it's getting in the way of your life in real, concrete ways. Here are signs it's time to loop in an adult:

! You're dreading going to school regularly (not just "Monday morning" dread — consistent, significant dread)

! Your sleep is badly affected most nights

! You're not eating, or eating much more than usual

! You're withdrawing from people and things you usually enjoy

! Physical symptoms (stomachaches, headaches, fatigue) happen frequently with no medical cause

! You feel like you can't control your anxiety or mood, no matter what you try

! You're having thoughts that scare you

Important: If you're having thoughts of hurting yourself, please tell a trusted adult today. Not tomorrow. Today. You don't have to handle that alone, and you don't have to wait until it gets worse.

Who to Talk To: Your Support Map

Think about the people in your life and where they fall on this map:

Tier 1: First reach (people closest to you)

- A parent or guardian who listens without immediately trying to fix everything
- An older sibling or cousin you trust
- A best friend who keeps things private

Tier 2: School support

- School counselor (this is literally their job—you don't need a crisis to go see them)
- A favorite teacher who has shown they care about students as people
- School psychologist (if your school has one)
- School nurse (a good first stop if you need a quiet moment)

Tier 3: Outside school

- A family friend, neighbor, or trusted community member
- A coach, club advisor, or religious leader, if applicable
- A therapist or counselor (your parents can help connect you if this feels right)

Fill in your personal support map:

My Tier 1 person: ____

My Tier 2 person at school: ______________________________________

Another person I could go to: _____________________________________

Scripts for Starting the Conversation

The hardest part of asking for help is often just finding the words to start. Here are some:

When you're stressed and overwhelmed:

"I've been feeling really stressed lately, and I'm not sure how to handle it. Can we talk?"

"I'm struggling with a lot right now. I don't need you to fix it—I just need someone to listen."

WHEN ANXIETY IS GETTING in the way:

"I've been really anxious about [school/friends/everything], and it's affecting my sleep and my focus. I think I might need some help figuring out how to manage it."

When you just need a break:

"I'm feeling really overwhelmed right now. Can I have a few minutes to step out?"

"I need a break. Can I go to the counselor's office for a bit?"

When you're not sure what's wrong:

"I don't even totally know what's going on, but I've been feeling off, and I think I need to talk to someone. Can that be you?"

You don't have to have it all figured out before you ask for help. "I don't know how to explain it, but I'm not okay" is a perfectly valid starting point.

Safe Break Zones at School

Sometimes you just need five minutes in a quiet place. Know these spots before you need them:

• **Counselor's office:** You can go here anytime. You don't need an appointment or a crisis. "I'm feeling overwhelmed and needed a few minutes" is enough.

• **Library:** Usually quiet, usually welcoming, and the librarian has seen students need a break before.

• **Nurse's office:** If you're feeling physically sick from anxiety (stomachache, headache), this is a legitimate stop.

• **A trusted teacher's classroom:** Before or after school, or during a free period. Some teachers are genuinely good at this.

• **A quiet bathroom:** Sometimes you just need two minutes alone with a cold water splash. That counts.

What to Do When You Can't Get Support Immediately

Sometimes you reach out, and the person isn't available right now. Or it's 10 PM, and you're spiraling, and there's no one to call. Here's your bridge plan:

• **Write it out:** In your Glow Up Journal or even just a notes app. Getting the spiral out of your head and onto a page gives your brain a tiny bit of relief.

• **The worry window:** Set a timer for 10 minutes. Allow yourself to worry freely during that window. When the timer goes off, close the window. You're not ignoring the problem—you're giving it a scheduled slot.

• **Distract with purpose:** Watch something funny, listen to music, call someone for a normal conversation. This isn't avoiding—it's giving your nervous system a break while you wait for the right support.

• **Crisis text line:** If you're in crisis and can't reach anyone, text HOME to 741741 (Crisis Text Line). Free, confidential, 24/7.

> "I texted my counselor once at the end of the day because I was spiraling about something and couldn't make it through the afternoon. She pulled me out of my next class for 15 minutes. Just talking it through was enough. I didn't know I could do that."
>
> — Sofia, 8th grade

Taking Care of Yourself: The Everyday Stuff That Actually Matters

This might be the least glamorous section in the whole book. No scripts, no flowcharts, no recovery moves. Just the basics—the foundational habits that either make everything else easier or make everything else harder. You already know most of this. But knowing it and actually doing it are very different things.

Sleep: The Non-Negotiable

Middle schoolers need 8–9 hours of sleep per night. Most get significantly less. And the effects aren't just tiredness—sleep deprivation directly impairs emotional regulation, memory, focus, and decision-making. When you're chronically underslept, your stress and anxiety levels are higher, you're more irritable, and the coping tools in this chapter are less effective.

This isn't a lecture. It's just physics. A tired brain is less resilient.

Small sleep improvements that actually work:

• Phone on Do Not Disturb or in another room 30 minutes before bed

• Same bedtime on weeknights (your body clock rewards consistency)

• A five-minute wind-down ritual: dim lights, one calm activity (reading, light stretching, slow music)

• If you can't fall asleep, try the 4-7-8 breath: in for 4, hold for 7, out for 8

• Pack your bag and pick your outfit the night before—one less thing to stress about in the morning

MOVEMENT: The Mood Reset Button

Exercise is one of the most well-researched mood boosters that exists. It releases endorphins, reduces cortisol (your stress hormone), and improves sleep. And you don't need a gym or a sports team to benefit from it.

Low-effort, high-impact movement options:

- A 10-minute walk after school before you start homework

- Three songs' worth of dancing in your room

- Shooting hoops, riding a bike, jumping on a trampoline

- YouTube yoga or stretching videos (10–15 minutes)

- A hallway lap between classes with actual intention behind it

The goal isn't fitness. The goal is to give your brain a chemical reset. Even 10 minutes makes a measurable difference in mood.

The "What Actually Helps Me" List

Everyone's reset looks different. Some people need social connections to recharge. Some need solitude. Some need physical movement. Some need creative output. Some need distraction, others need to process.

Build your personal list:

Things that reliably improve my mood:

1.

____

2.

____

3.

____

Things I reach for that actually make me feel worse:

1.

____

2.

____

The one thing I can always do when nothing else sounds good:

____

The goal: When you're in a low mood, you won't want to think of what to do. Having this list written down means you don't have to—you just look at it and pick one.

Big Feelings Glow Up Tracker

This tracker is specifically for noticing your emotional patterns, your go-to tools, and your growth in managing hard feelings over time.

Week of:

____

MY MOOD THIS WEEK (circle one for each day):

Mon: 😄 Great 😐 Okay 😟 Rough 😣 Really hard

Tue: 😄 Great 😐 Okay 😟 Rough 😣 Really hard

Wed: 😄 Great 😐 Okay 😟 Rough 😣 Really hard

Thu: 😄 Great 😐 Okay 😟 Rough 😣 Really hard

Fri: 😄 Great 😐 Okay 😟 Rough 😣 Really hard

BIGGEST FEELING THIS WEEK:

What emotion showed up most? What triggered it?

____

____

TOOL I USED:

Which calming strategy, mindfulness hack, or coping move did I try?

____

DID IT HELP? (circle): Yes   Somewhat   Not really   Didn't try one

WHO I TALKED TO (if anyone):

____

ONE THING I'M PROUD OF EMOTIONALLY THIS WEEK:

(Kept it together in a tough moment, asked for help, named a feeling instead of acting it out, let something go, etc.)

____

____

____

EMOTIONAL RESILIENCE CHECK:

How well did I handle my big feelings this week?

1 ---- 2 ---- 3 ---- 4 ---- 5 ---- 6 ---- 7 ---- 8 ---- 9 ---- 10

Monthly Reflection

• What emotion showed up most this month? What does that tell me?

• Which calming tool has been most reliable for me?

• When did I ask for help this month? How did that go?

• What's one situation I handled better than I would have three months ago?

• What's one area of emotional health I want to focus on next month?

Your Feelings Are Information, Not the Enemy

Here's what you now have:

• An understanding of why middle school feelings are so intense (and why that's normal)

• A mood tracker to spot your patterns

• The 5-4-3-2-1 grounding exercise, the anchor breath, and other mini-mindfulness tools

• Panic plans for tests, presentations, and social drama—including invisible techniques for the middle of class

• A personal support map so you know exactly who to turn to

• Scripts for asking for help, even when you don't know what to say

• A bridge plan for hard moments when support isn't immediately available

• The basics—sleep and movement—and why they matter more than any app

Your feelings are not weaknesses. They're information. Stress tells you something matters. Anxiety tells you your brain is trying to protect you. Sadness tells you something needs attention. Irritability tells you something is off. The goal isn't to stop feeling—it's to get good enough at working with your feelings that they don't run your whole day.

You're getting there. One hard day at a time.

self-esteem and identity—liking yourself irl and online

Here's a question nobody asks out loud, but almost everyone wonders in middle school: Who am I, actually?

Not "what's my name and where do I live"—you've had that figured out for a while. More like: What do I actually like, separate from what my friends like? What kind of person do I want to be? Why does it feel so hard to just... be myself? And why does scrolling through other people's lives make me feel like I'm somehow falling behind in a race I didn't sign up for?

This chapter is about all of that. Identity. Self-esteem. The comparison trap. Body changes nobody warned you about clearly enough. The pressure to blend in vs. the deep human need to stand out. And the quiet, essential work of learning to talk to yourself like someone you actually like.

None of this gets fully figured out in middle school. But middle school is where the work begins. And starting it here, on purpose, puts you so far ahead of where most people start.

The Comparison Trap—How to Stop Measuring Yourself Against Others

Let's start with one of the most universal middle school experiences: seeing someone else—their grades, their body, their friend group, their highlight reel on social media—and immediately feeling like you come up short.

Comparison is human. It's actually a brain function that evolved to help us understand our social standing. But in middle school, with a phone that delivers a constant stream of curated "best moments" from dozens of people simultaneously, comparison has become a sport with no finish line and no winners.

Why Comparison Feels So Much Worse Now

A few things make comparison especially painful at this age:

- **Your identity is still forming.** When you don't have a fully settled sense of who you are yet, it's easy to measure yourself against others as a way of figuring out where you fit. But it's a shaky measuring stick.
- **Social media shows highlight reels, not real life.** The photos people post are the best versions of moments that probably had boring, awkward, or messy parts you never see. You're comparing your full, unfiltered reality to someone else's greatest hits.
- **Middle school magnifies status.** Popularity, appearance, and social standing feel like enormous stakes right now. That's partly biology —your brain is wired to care intensely about belonging at this age. But it also means comparison hits harder.
- **Everyone's developing at different rates.** Some people look older. Some are already in relationships. Some got taller over the summer. Development timelines vary widely, and comparisons make those differences feel like deficits. They aren't.

The Reality Behind the Feed: What You're Actually Comparing To

Let's pull back the curtain on what a social media post actually represents:

What you see: *A friend's perfect beach photo —glowing skin, great hair, beautiful sunset.*

What you don't see: The seventeen photos taken before that one. The editing app is used to smooth and brighten. The argument they had with their family that morning. The sunburn they got right after. The anxiety about whether people would like it.

What you see: *Someone's amazing birthday party with fifty friends and a gorgeous setup.*

What you don't see: That those fifty people are acquaintances, not close friends. That the setup was their mom's doing. That they cried for an hour before guests arrived because they were worried nobody would come.

This isn't about saying other people's lives are miserable. It's about recognizing that everyone's life has the same ratio of good moments to hard moments —the feed just only shows you one side of that ratio.

> "I used to follow this girl who always looked perfect.
> Perfect skin, perfect style, always doing something
> cool. One day in school I saw her crying in the
> bathroom over something her boyfriend said. She
> looked completely different from her feed. I
> unfollowed her after that—not to be mean, just
> because it wasn't doing me any good."

— Jasmine, 8th grade

Practical Strategies for Breaking the Comparison Habit

The Unfollow/Mute Challenge:

Go through who you follow. Ask yourself honestly: Does seeing this person's content make me feel inspired, connected, or happy—or does it make me feel bad about myself? You are allowed to unfollow or mute accounts that consistently make you feel worse. This is not petty. It is self-care.

The "Five Good Things" Self-Check:

When you catch yourself comparing unfavorably, interrupt it. Pull out your phone or a piece of paper and write five specific things about yourself that are genuinely good. Not generic ("I'm nice")—specific. "I remembered my friend's hard week and texted to check in." "I got through that presentation even though I was terrified." "I'm really good at knowing when something is funny."

You're not dismissing the comparison. You're redirecting your brain to evidence of your own value.

1. The "Comparison Pause": The moment you notice you're comparing yourself to someone, say in your head: "I'm comparing right now." Just naming it—like the name-it move from Chapter 7—takes some of its power away. Then ask: What do I actually know about their full life? Usually, the honest answer is: not much.

2. Your Journey, Your Pace: Different people develop different things at different times. The person who seems to have it all together socially right now might be struggling with something invisible. The person who seems "behind" academically might be developing a creative or emotional intelligence that doesn't show up on a test. Everybody's timeline is their own.

3. Glow Up Tracker Prompt: This week, notice every time you catch yourself comparing. Just tally marks. Don't judge it—just count it. At the end of the week, look at the number. Awareness is the first step.

4. "Is My Body Weird?"—Handling Body Changes and Online Filters

Nobody's body goes through puberty on a schedule. Some people hit it early, some late, some in between. Some people shoot up six inches in one summer. Others don't until high school. Bodies change at their own pace, in their own order, and no two people's experience is the same.

What IS the same: Almost everyone feels weird about their body at some point during middle school. That awkward, uncomfortable, "is this normal?" feeling is one of the most shared experiences of this age group, even though people rarely say it out loud.

5. What's Actually Happening (Without Being Weird About It)

Here's a plain-language overview of what puberty involves, because nobody should be caught off guard:

- **Growth spurts:** Rapid increases in height, sometimes so fast your joints ache. Your body is growing faster than it can fully keep up with—that's normal.
- **Body shape changes:** Hips widening, shoulders broadening, muscle development, or fat redistribution. Bodies come in all shapes and sizes, and the variation during puberty is enormous.
- **Skin changes:** Increased oil production leads to breakouts. Acne is not a hygiene failure. It is a hormonal reality, and it happens to the vast majority of people at this age.
- **Body odor:** New sweat glands are activating. Completely normal, easily managed with deodorant. Not a crisis.
- **Voice changes:** Most pronounced in people assigned male at birth, but everyone's voice shifts somewhat. Cracks happen. They stop.
- **Hair growth:** In new places. Totally normal. How you choose to manage or not manage it is entirely your call.
- **Emotional intensity:** Already covered in Chapter 7—but yes, it's connected to the same biological changes.

The most important thing to know: There is no "right" age or pace for any of this. Early, late, fast, slow—all of it is within the range of normal. If you have specific concerns, a doctor is a judgment-free resource.

Fact or Cap: Puberty Edition

Let's bust some myths:

FACT OR CAP: "If you get acne, you're not washing your face enough."

CAP. Acne is caused primarily by hormones, not dirt. Over-washing can actually make it worse by drying out your skin and triggering more oil production. A gentle cleanser once or twice a day is plenty.

FACT OR CAP: "You should have hit your growth spurt by now."

CAP. Growth spurts happen between ages 9 and 17. If you haven't had yours yet, it doesn't mean something is wrong. It means your body is on its own timeline.

FACT OR CAP: "If you sweat, you smell."

Mostly cap. Sweat itself is mostly odorless. It's the bacteria on your skin interacting with sweat that creates odor. Applying deodorant or antiperspirant to clean skin reliably solves this.

FACT OR CAP: "Everybody in the movies and on social media is what a normal body looks like."

Hard cap. Media bodies are filtered, edited, professionally lit, selected for a specific look, and often digitally altered. The range of "normal" human bodies is vastly wider and more diverse than any screen suggests.

FACT OR CAP: "Once puberty starts, your body will just keep changing forever."

Cap. Puberty is a phase, not a permanent state. Most people's bodies settle into a more stable place by their mid-to-late teens.

Filters, Editing Apps, and the Body Image Trap

Social media filters and editing apps can change the shape of your face, smooth your skin, enlarge your eyes, slim your waist, and alter your appearance in ways that are nearly undetectable to the casual viewer. Many of the "bodies" and "faces" you see online do not exist in the unfiltered world.

> "I spent like two years trying to figure out why my skin never looked like my favorite influencer's skin. Turns out she uses three different filters AND editing software on every single post. I felt kind of dumb for not realizing it, but also kind of furious."
>
> — Destiny, 8th grade

This isn't about blaming people who use filters—lots of people do, for lots of reasons. It's about being a smart consumer of the images you see. When you see a body or face that seems impossibly perfect, the honest question is: Is this real, or is this produced?

Practical Self-Care and Body Confidence

Body confidence isn't about loving everything about your appearance at all times—that's not realistic for most adults, let alone middle schoolers going through puberty. It's about treating your body with basic respect and finding things it can do that you appreciate.

Simple basics that actually help:

✓ Consistent sleep (skin heals itself during sleep—this is not a myth)

✓ Staying hydrated (water genuinely affects skin, energy, and mood)

✓ Moving your body in ways that feel good to you (not punishing, not performative—just movement)

✓ Wearing clothes that fit your actual body, not the body you think you should have

✓ Deodorant, a simple face wash routine, and dental hygiene—the basics that make you feel physically comfortable in your skin

A reframe that actually sticks:

Instead of "Do I like how this looks?" try asking: "What can my body DO that I'm grateful for?"

It carried me through that presentation when my legs were shaking

It let me laugh until I couldn't breathe

It kept going through a hard practice, even when I wanted to quit

It gets me where I need to go every day

Journal Prompt: One thing my body can do that I'm genuinely grateful for:

____

____

____

Celebrating What Makes You Unique (Without Feeling "Extra")

Here's the tension that almost every middle schooler feels: You want to fit in AND stand out. You want to belong to a group AND be recognized as an individual. You want people to like you, AND you don't want to change yourself to make that happen.

That tension is real. It doesn't fully resolve in middle school. But here's what's also true: The things that make you different from everyone else are the things that will eventually become your greatest strengths—in friendships, in work, in the kind of life you build.

The goal isn't to be loud about your uniqueness if that doesn't feel safe. It's to stop treating it as a problem.

Exploring Your Identity: The Big Questions

Identity is built gradually, through trying things, noticing what feels right, and letting go of what doesn't. Here are some questions to sit with—not to answer perfectly, but to start exploring:

- What do I do that makes me lose track of time?
- What topics do I get genuinely excited about, even if they're not "cool"?
- What do I believe about how people should treat each other?
- What parts of my family background or culture am I curious about or proud of?
- Who are the people I feel most like myself around?
- What's something I'm good at that I rarely talk about?
- If I could spend a whole Saturday doing anything, what would it be?
- What do I stand for, even when it's unpopular?

These questions don't need to be answered today or all at once. They're worth returning to over the next few years. Your answers will change as you do.

> "I was really into model trains. Like, genuinely obsessed. I never told anyone at school because I thought they'd think it was weird. Then I mentioned it once in art class, and two people got excited because they'd never met anyone who knew about it. We ended up hanging out. The weird thing was actually the thing."
>
> — Ben, 7th grade

Low-Key Self-Expression: Being Yourself Without a Spotlight

You don't have to make a grand announcement about who you are. Self-expression can be quiet and personal:

Pins and patches: On your backpack, jacket, or bag. A small visual shorthand for things you care about that invites conversation from the right people.

Your playlist: The music you choose says something about you. You don't have to share it, but you can—and sometimes it connects you with people you didn't expect.

Your online bio or profile: A few specific words about who you are. Not generic ("I like music") — specific ("I listen to 70s funk and I make stop-motion videos").

How you decorate your space: Your locker, your room, your notebook covers. Your space reflects you without you having to say a word.

The causes you show up for: Joining a club, volunteering, standing up for something you believe in — these are expressions of identity in action.

Handling Teasing or Questions About What Makes You Different

When you express something genuine about yourself, sometimes people respond with confusion, jokes, or questions. Here's how to handle it without shrinking:

> *"Yeah, it's a little different, but I genuinely love it."*
>
> *"It's not for everyone, but it's definitely for me."*
>
> *"I know it's kind of niche — but the people who get it really get it."*
>
> *"Want to know more about it? I could talk about this for hours."*

These responses do something important: They own the thing without being defensive or apologetic. You're not asking permission to like what you like. You're just liking it.

Celebrating Diversity in the People Around You

One of the most powerful things about middle school is that you're suddenly surrounded by people from different backgrounds, with different experiences, interests, and perspectives. That's not a complication — it's an opportunity.

Challenge: Find someone in your school who has a completely different interest, background, or perspective from you. Ask them one genuine question about it. Not to be polite — because you're actually curious. "How did you get into that?" or "What do you love about it?"

You might be surprised by what you discover. About them, and about yourself.

"No Cap" Self-Talk — How to Reframe Negative Thoughts AFK and Online

Your inner voice is talking constantly. And for most middle schoolers, a significant portion of what it says is unkind. Not out of meanness — out of habit, fear, and the deeply human tendency to be harder on yourself than you would ever be on a friend.

This section is about noticing that voice, questioning it, and gradually replacing the harshest parts with something more honest and fair. Not toxic positivity. Not pretending everything is great. Just... treating yourself with the same basic decency you'd give someone you care about.

How Negative Self-Talk Sneaks In

It's rarely a dramatic voice screaming insults. It's quieter than that:

"Why did I say that? That was so stupid." (after a conversation that didn't go perfectly)

"I'm so awkward. Nobody else is this awkward." (not true, but feels true)

"That person is so much better at this than me." (maybe, in this one area, right now — but so what?)

"I'll never be good at this." (based on limited evidence, ignoring all the times you improved at something)

"They probably think I'm weird." (mind-reading, almost always inaccurate)

"I'm not as pretty/smart/funny/cool as..." (the comparison trap in self-talk form)

Social media adds a whole extra layer: seeing a post with no likes, getting fewer comments than someone else, and reading a comment that stings. Digital spaces deliver tiny doses of comparison and rejection constantly, and each one can trigger a spiral of negative self-talk if you're not paying attention.

The "Would You Say This to a Friend?" Test

This is the simplest and most effective self-talk check:

Take the thing you just said to yourself and imagine saying it out loud to your best friend.

"You said something dumb in class. You're so embarrassing."

Would you say that to a friend who had an awkward moment? Of course not. You'd say: "Hey, everyone has moments like that. It's not a big deal."

"You look weird today."

Would you say that to a friend? Never. So why is it okay to say it to yourself?

The standard you hold yourself to doesn't have to be perfect — but it should at minimum meet the standard you'd hold for someone you love. That's not self-indulgence. That's basic fairness.

The "Flip It" Exercise

For every harsh self-thought, practice flipping it to something more realistic and kind. Not fake-positive—genuinely true and fair:

❌ **Harsh:** *"I messed up that presentation. I'm so bad at public speaking."*

✅ **Flip:** *"I had a rough presentation. I'm still learning how to do this. Every time I do it, I get a little better."*

❌ **Harsh:** *"No one responded to my message. Nobody actually likes me."*

✅ **Flip:** *"People get busy and miss messages. One unanswered text is not a verdict on whether I'm likeable."*

❌ **Harsh:** *"I'm the only one who doesn't know what they're doing."*

✅ **Flip:** *"Most people feel uncertain about what they're doing right now. I'm not alone in this."*

❌ **Harsh:** *"I'm not as [anything] as [person]."*

✅ **Flip:** *"We're different people on different paths. Their strengths don't cancel out mine."*

Your turn:

A thought I say to myself often:

____

____

A fairer and more realistic version:

____

____

Digital Self-Kindness: How You Talk to Yourself Online

Self-talk doesn't just happen in your head—it shows up in what you post, what you comment, and how you respond to your own content online. Here are some ways to practice digital self-kindness:

• **Post what you actually like, not just what you think will get likes.**
When you post something that's genuinely you—a passion, a joke, something you made—you feel better about it regardless of how many people respond. When you post something calculated to get approval, you're tying your self-worth to a number.

- **Detach from metrics.** Likes and views are data about what the algorithm promotes, not votes on your value as a person. They are genuinely unrelated to how worthy you are of love, friendship, and belonging.

- **Leave kind comments.** The act of genuinely complimenting someone else's post—not performatively, but because you mean it—shifts your brain from consuming to contributing. It feels better than scrolling.

- **Don't post when you're upset.** Venting online rarely feels as good as you hope and almost always has unintended consequences. Write it in your Glow Up Journal instead. Then decide if you still want to post.

The "No Cap" Self-Affirmation Ritual

Affirmations have a reputation for being cheesy. That's because vague ones are. "I am beautiful and worthy of love" feels hollow if you don't believe it yet. But specific, evidence-based affirmations are different. These aren't wishes—they're true statements:

"I showed up to school today even though it was hard. That took something."

"I kept trying at [subject] even when it felt impossible. That's real."

"I noticed when my friend was struggling and reached out. That's the kind of person I am."

"I said something brave today. It didn't go perfectly, but I said it."

Your "No Cap" affirmation isn't about who you want to be someday. It's about seeing clearly who you already are, right now.

Your weekly "No Cap" statement (fill in):

One real, specific thing I like about myself this week:

____

____

One way I showed up for someone else this week:

____

One hard thing I did that I'm not giving myself enough credit for:

____

Self-Esteem and Identity Glow Up Tracker

Your sense of self is not fixed. It's something you actively build through the way you think about yourself, how you treat your body, and what you choose to express out loud. This tracker helps you notice that building in real time.

Week of:

____

COMPARISON CHECK:

How many times did I catch myself comparing this week? (No judgment—just notice)

Tally: _________   What triggered it most? _______________________

SELF-TALK AUDIT:

The harshest thing I said to myself this week:

____

The fairer version I could have said:

____

UNIQUENESS WIN:

One thing I expressed or owned about myself this week (interest, opinion, background, etc.):

____

____

MY "NO CAP" STATEMENT THIS WEEK:

One real, specific thing I'm giving myself credit for:

____

____

DIGITAL SELF-KINDNESS CHECK:

Did I scroll in a way that made me feel worse about myself this week?

☐ Yes ☐ No ☐ A little bit

What's one thing I could do differently next week?

____

SELF-ESTEEM CONFIDENCE CHECK:

How clearly am I seeing my own value this week?

1 ---- 2 ---- 3 ---- 4 ---- 5 ---- 6 ---- 7 ---- 8 ----- 9 ---- 10

Monthly Reflection

• How has my self-talk shifted since I started paying attention to it?

• What's one thing about myself I've started to appreciate that I used to ignore or dislike?

• What's one part of my identity I feel more comfortable expressing than I did a month ago?

• Whose comparison trap am I most likely to fall into? What do I want to do about that?

• What's one "No Cap" truth about myself that I want to carry into next month?

You Are Already Someone Worth Knowing

Here's what you now have:

• A clear-eyed understanding of why comparison feels so intense right now —and practical strategies for interrupting it

• Honest, non-awkward information about body changes and what's actually normal

• Tools for seeing through filtered and edited online images

A framework for exploring and expressing your identity at whatever pace feels right

• Scripts for handling teasing or questions about what makes you different

• The "Flip It" exercise and the "Would You Say This to a Friend?" test for kinder self-talk

• The "No Cap" affirmation practice—specific, evidence-based, and actually believable

• A digital self-kindness framework for how you show up online

Here's the thing about identity: You don't find it. You build it. Slowly, imperfectly, through trying things and noticing what fits, through making mistakes and choosing how to respond, through showing up for people and letting people show up for you. Middle school is just the beginning of that building project—and you're already further along than you think.

nine
digital life mastery— social media, privacy, and staying safe online

You live in two worlds simultaneously: the one you walk through every day—hallways, cafeteria, classrooms—and the digital one you carry in your pocket. Both worlds are real. Both have social rules, consequences, and opportunities. And both require skills that don't come automatically.

The difference is that your offline mistakes are usually witnessed by a small number of people and fade with time. Your online mistakes can be screenshotted, shared, and permanently attached to your name in ways that follow you further than you'd ever expect. That's not meant to be scary—it's just true, and knowing it helps you make smarter decisions.

This chapter covers the skills nobody officially teaches you: what to post and what to hold back, how to protect your privacy, how to manage your digital footprint, and how to spot and shut down suspicious behavior before it becomes a real problem.

(Quick note: If you want a refresher on group chat dynamics, drama, and how to handle digital exclusion specifically, Chapter 3 has you covered. This chapter zooms out to the bigger picture of your overall digital life.)

Social Media Drama: What to Post, What to Ghost, and How to Handle Comments

Every post you make is a decision. Most people don't treat it that way—they post impulsively, emotionally, or just because everyone else is. But the people who navigate social media well are the ones who pause before they post and ask a few key questions.

The Pause Before You Post: Three Questions

Before you post anything—a photo, a caption, a comment, a story—run through these:

Question 1: Would I say this in person?

If you wouldn't walk up to someone in the cafeteria and say it to their face, you probably shouldn't put it in writing either. The distance of a screen makes things feel less real, but the impact is just as real, often more, because it can be screenshotted and shared.

Question 2: Would I be okay if my teacher, parent, or coach saw this?

You might think "they're never going to see it." But things travel in unexpected directions. A screenshot ends up somewhere you didn't anticipate. Someone shows it to the wrong person. The internet has a long memory. If you'd be uncomfortable with a specific trusted adult seeing it, that's worth paying attention to.

Question 3: Is this kind—or at least neutral?

This doesn't mean every post has to be a motivational quote. You can be funny, sarcastic, and real. But there's a line between humor and cruelty, between venting and targeting someone. If the post would make a specific person feel hurt, embarrassed, or unsafe, it crosses that line.

The 24-hour rule for emotional posts: If you're upset and you want to post about it, write the post in your notes app. Wait 24 hours. Read it again. If you still want to post it—and it passes the three questions above—go ahead. Most of the time, you won't want to anymore.

Navigating Likes, Comments, and the Approval Loop

Here's something worth understanding about how social media is designed: Every app is built to keep you coming back. Likes, comments, follower counts, view numbers—these features are engineered to trigger the same reward pathways in your brain as a slot machine. A notification delivers a tiny hit of dopamine. No notification delivers a tiny hit of anxiety. This is intentional design, not coincidence.

Knowing this doesn't make you immune to it. But it helps you see what's actually happening when you feel that anxious pull to check whether your post got likes.

What to do when a post gets fewer responses than you hoped:

1. Remind yourself: engagement metrics are about algorithms, timing, and chance—not your worth

2. Notice the feeling without acting on it (don't delete, don't repost, don't fish for compliments)
3. Ask honestly: Did I post this because I genuinely wanted to share it, or because I wanted validation? Both are human, but knowing which one helps you understand your relationship with the platform

Handling negative or "salty" comments:

"Thanks for sharing your thoughts." [No further engagement. Don't feed it.]

"I appreciate your opinion." [Disarming without agreeing or escalating.]

No response at all. Sometimes the best answer is silence. A comment left without a reaction quickly loses its power.

When to delete a comment vs. report it:

1. **Delete:** Mildly rude or annoying, not threatening or targeting anyone
2. **Report:** Harassing, threatening, discriminatory, or repeatedly targeting you even after you've asked them to stop
3. **Block:** Anyone whose presence in your comments or DMs consistently makes you feel uncomfortable or unsafe — no explanation needed, no drama required

When a Friend Is Upset About Not Being Tagged

This is genuinely tricky because it sits at the intersection of digital life and real friendship. Here's how to handle it:

"Hey, I wasn't trying to leave you out — I posted that one quickly and didn't think about tagging everyone. I'm sorry it hurt your feelings."

"I'll tag you next time. I didn't realize it would matter to you."

If it keeps being an issue, the real conversation is about the friendship, not the tagging. "Hey, it seems like you've been bothered by some of my posts lately. Can we talk about what's actually going on?"

Using Social Media for Something That Actually Feels Good

Social media gets a lot of bad press, and some of it is deserved. But it's also genuinely useful for connection, creativity, and finding your people. Here are ways to use it that tend to feel good rather than bad:

☑ **Post what you actually care about—not what you think will perform.** The posts you're most proud of are usually the ones that felt most like you.

☑ **Use it to learn.** Follow accounts about things you're genuinely interested in—art, science, animals, history, whatever. Let the algorithm work for you.

☑ **Connect intentionally.** Use it to stay close to people you actually care about—not to collect followers or manage an image.

☑ **Create.** Make stuff. Art, videos, playlists, and photos that you take because you like them. Creating feels fundamentally different from just consuming.

☑ **Leave kind comments.** Not performatively—genuinely. When something makes you smile, say so. It shifts your role from passive consumer to active contributor, and it feels better.

Challenge: Post a compliment or a genuinely positive comment on someone else's content three days in a row. Notice how it feels compared to scrolling and comparing.

Private vs. Public—Keeping Your Stuff Safe on the Internet

Privacy isn't just about strangers on the internet. It's about controlling your own information—who has access to it, what they can do with it, and what trail you're leaving behind. Most people don't think about this until something goes wrong. This section is about thinking about it before anything does.

The "Never Share" List

These are non-negotiables. No exceptions, no matter how much you trust the person you're talking to online:

🚫 **Your full name + school name together.** Either one alone is manageable. Together, they allow someone to physically locate you.

🚫 **Your home address or specific neighborhood.** Even something as vague as "I live near [landmark]" provides more information than a stranger needs.

🚫 **Your phone number to someone you've only met online.** Even if they seem completely trustworthy.

🚫 **Your passwords.** To anyone. Ever. Including close friends. Friendships change, and access to your accounts is a serious vulnerability.

🚫 **Your daily schedule or location patterns.** "I walk home the same way every day at 3:30" is more specific than you might realize.

🚫 **Anything your family is doing.** Travel plans, being home alone, and family situations can change—this information can be used in ways you wouldn't anticipate.

🚫 **Photos of yourself that feel uncomfortable to share.** Once something is sent, you lose complete control of it. This applies to photos of any kind.

Real-Life Scenario: When Oversharing Has Consequences

> "I was in an online gaming community, and I mentioned my school name in a chat without thinking. Someone I'd never met started showing up in conversations with very specific details about things at my school. It was really unsettling. I had to leave the whole community and change my username. I never figured out who it was."
>
> — Anonymous, 8th grade

This kind of thing doesn't just happen in dramatic movies. It happens in ordinary gaming chats, fan communities, and comment sections. The information you share casually adds up.

Understanding Your Digital Footprint

Your digital footprint is the trail of data you leave behind every time you use the internet. It includes everything you've posted, commented on, liked, searched for, or signed up for. Some of it is visible. Some of it is invisible, but still being collected. All of it is more permanent than most people realize.

The permanence problem:

⚠ Deleting a post removes it from your profile but not from screenshots others have taken

⚠ Deleted messages may still exist on the other person's device or in app servers

⚠ Anything posted publicly has potentially been indexed by search engines

⚠ Even "temporary" content like stories can be screen-recorded

The reputation problem:

High schools, colleges, and employers increasingly search applicants' names online. What you post now could be findable years from now. This isn't meant to paralyze you—you don't have to curate a perfect personal brand. It just means that the question "Would I be okay if this lived online for the next five years?" is worth asking.

THE ACTIVITY: Google yourself.

Right now, or the next time you have access to a computer. Search for your full name. Search for your username. See what comes up. If anything surprises you, that's good information to have.

Privacy Settings & Blocking: Digital Defense Checkup

Privacy settings are reset sometimes when apps update. Make it a habit to check yours every few months. Here's a quick guide:

Instagram:

☑ Settings → Privacy → Account Privacy: Set to Private
☑ Settings → Privacy → Story: Choose who can reply and who can share your stories
☑ Settings → Privacy → Tags: Manually approve tags before they appear on your profile
☑ Settings → Privacy → Mentions: Limit who can mention you
☑ Settings → Messages → Message Requests: Control who can DM you
☑ Settings → Privacy → Comments: restrict who can comment
☑ To block: go to their profile, tap •••, select Block

TikTok:
☑ Settings → Privacy: Set account to Private
☑ Settings → Privacy → Safety: Turn off "Suggest your account to others"
☑ Settings → Privacy → Direct Messages: Set to 'Friends only', 'Off' or 'Restrict'
☑ Settings → Privacy → Duet/Stitch: Limit to Friends if you don't want strangers using your content
☑ Settings → Privacy → Downloads: Turn off to prevent others from saving your videos
☑ Settings → Privacy → Comments: filter or turn off
☑ To block: long-press their comment or go to their profile and select Block

Snapchat:

☑ Settings → Privacy Controls → Contact Me: Set to My Friends
☑ Settings → Privacy Controls → View My Story: Set to My Friends
☑ Settings → Privacy Controls → See My Location: Turn off or set to select friends only via Snap Map
☑ Settings → Privacy Controls → See Me in Quick Add: Turn off
☑ To block: press and hold on their name → Manage Friendship → Block

Discord:

☑ User Settings → Set your profile to Friends Only or Private
☑ User Settings → Privacy & Safety: Enable "Safe Direct Messaging"
☑ User Settings → Privacy & Safety: Turn off "Allow DMs from server members" for servers where you don't know everyone
☑ Server Settings: In each server, check your nickname and what's visible to other members
☑ To block: click their username → three dots → Block

Gaming platforms (Xbox, PlayStation, Steam, etc.):

☑ Turn off location sharing if it's a feature
☑ Review who can see your activity and what games you're playing
☑ Disable direct messages from non-friends
☑ Reporting a user sends their behavior to the platform's safety team. It's not tattling. It's using the tools that exist for exactly this reason.
☑ Blocking doesn't notify the person that you blocked them. They just can't reach you anymore.
☑ Muting is quieter than blocking and works well for low-level situations.

Monthly reminder: Set a reminder in your phone for the first of every month: "Check privacy settings." Takes five minutes. Worth it every time.

Protecting Your Accounts: Passwords and Two-Factor Authentication

Strong password basics:

✔ At least 12 characters, mixing letters, numbers, and symbols

✔ Different password for each important account (email, social media, gaming)

✔ Never use obvious personal info: your name, birthday, pet's name, school name

✔ A password manager app (like Bitwarden, free) stores them all so you only have to remember one

Two-factor authentication (2FA):

When you enable 2FA, logging in requires both your password AND a code sent to your phone. This means even if someone gets your password, they can't access your account without your phone, too. Enable it on every account that offers it—especially email, which is the key to everything else.

How to spot a phishing attempt:

⚠ An email or DM claiming to be from a platform, asking you to "verify your account" by clicking a link

! The link URL looks slightly off ("instagramm.com" instead of "instagram.com")

! The message creates urgency: "Your account will be deleted in 24 hours!"

! Rule: Never click a link in an email or DM asking for your login info. Go directly to the app or website instead.

Spotting Red Flags—How to Handle Online Strangers and "Sus" Behavior

Most people you interact with online are exactly who they say they are. But not all of them. And the ones who aren't are often very good at seeming normal—at first. Learning to recognize warning signs early is one of the most important safety skills of the digital age.

The Red Flag Checklist: Sus Behavior to Watch For

Be on alert if someone online does any of the following:

▶ **Moves very fast.** They go from hello to "you're my best friend" in a few days. They want to talk constantly and get upset when you're unavailable.

▶ **Asks for personal information early.** Your school, your address, your phone number, what you look like, and where you hang out.

▶ **Wants to move the conversation off-platform.** "DM me on Snapchat instead" or "Text me at this number"—especially from someone you don't know in real life. Moving platforms makes the conversation harder to trace.

▶ **Gives excessive compliments.** "You're so mature for your age." "I've never met anyone like you." "You're so much more interesting than kids my age." These are grooming patterns, not genuine friendship.

▶ **Asks you to keep the conversation secret.** "Don't tell your parents about us." "This is just between you and me." Any adult who asks a young person to keep a relationship secret from their parents has bad intentions.

▶ **Sends unsolicited photos or asks for them.** Especially photos of your body, your face, or your home environment.

▶ **Claims to be a peer, but something feels off.** The profile looks too perfect, has very few posts, no real friends in common, or the details about their life keep changing.

▶ **Makes you feel guilty for having boundaries.** "If you really trusted me, you'd tell me." "I thought we were friends." Healthy relationships—online or off—respect your boundaries.

Trust your gut. If something feels off, it probably is. You don't need to be able to explain exactly why. That uncomfortable feeling is information, not paranoia.

Catfishing: What It Is and How to Spot It

Catfishing is when someone creates a fake online identity to deceive you. They might use stolen photos, a made-up name, a fake age, and a fabricated life story. It happens more often than most people think, and not just to naive or inexperienced users—it happens to people who consider themselves pretty savvy online.

Signs a profile might be fake:

- Very few posts, all posted within a short time frame

- Photos look like professional modeling shots or are suspiciously perfect

- No mutual friends or connections to anyone you know in real life

- Their story has inconsistencies—age, location, school, or life details that don't add up

- They avoid video calls or real-time photos, always with an excuse

- They claim to have a dramatic backstory that conveniently creates sympathy

How to verify:

✓ Ask for a video call. Someone using stolen photos can't video chat as that person.

✓ Do a reverse image search: Save one of their photos, go to images.google.com, drag the photo in. If it appears on other accounts with a different name, it's stolen.

✓ Ask specific questions about things they've mentioned. Real people can answer details. Fabricated identities often contradict themselves.

> "I was in a fan community and made friends with someone who seemed my age. We talked for months. When I finally asked to video chat, they made a bunch of excuses. I reverse-image-searched their profile photo and found it on a modeling website under a completely different name. I felt so stupid, but my older sister said even adults fall for this. I reported the account and blocked them."
>
> — Anonymous, 7th grade

SCRIPTS FOR RESPONDING TO 'SUS' Behavior

If someone asks for personal information:

"I don't share that kind of information online."

"That's not something I'm comfortable sharing."

You don't owe an explanation. "I don't do that" is a complete sentence.

If they pressure you to move platforms or keep things secret:

"I'm good at keeping our conversations here."

"I don't keep my online friendships secret from my parents."

If you've realized something is wrong and want to exit:

"I'm not going to be continuing this conversation."

Then block. Then tell a trusted adult. In that order. You don't need to explain yourself to someone who has given you red flags.

Report, Block, Tell: The Three Steps That Always Apply

1. Report the account or content to the platform. It doesn't matter if you think it will do anything—reporting creates a record and contributes to the platform's safety systems.

2. Block the person. This removes their access to you immediately. It doesn't notify them with a specific message—you just disappear from their access.

3. Tell a trusted adult. This is not optional. Even if you're embarrassed. Even if you think it's "not a big deal." An adult needs to know. If the situation involves threats, explicit content, or someone who knows your personal information, tell an adult today and consider involving law enforcement.

Zero blame policy: If something uncomfortable happened online, it is not your fault for being friendly, for sharing something, or for not recognizing the signs earlier. People who engage in this behavior are skilled at manipulation. Telling an adult is not tattling. It's protecting yourself and potentially protecting the next person this happens to.

Your Digital Reputation: Building Something You're Proud Of

We've spent a lot of this chapter on protection and avoidance. Let's end with something more forward-looking: You have the ability to actively build a digital presence that reflects who you actually are and that you'll be proud of years from now.

This isn't about becoming an influencer or curating a perfect brand. It's about being intentional—posting with purpose, engaging with kindness, and leaving an online trail you'd be comfortable with your future self seeing.

The Digital Reputation Test

Imagine yourself at 18, applying for a summer job or a program you really want. The person reviewing your application googles your name. What do they find?

Best case: Evidence of your interests and passions, positive interactions with others, nothing that raises red flags.

Worst case: Mean comments, drama, embarrassing posts, or content that makes you look careless or unkind.

Most common case: Nothing, or not much. Which is actually fine, and better than the worst case.

You're not too young to start thinking about this. Not because you need to market yourself online—but because the habits you build now around what you post and how you engage become automatic over time. Build good habits now.

Being a Positive Digital Citizen

Digital citizenship isn't just about protecting yourself—it's about how you show up in online spaces for other people:

- **Call out, don't pile on.** If you see someone being targeted or harassed online, you can say something without joining a mob. "That's not okay" is enough.
- **Don't screenshot and spread.** Screenshots of someone's embarrassing moment, private conversation, or vulnerable post are almost never okay to share. If you wouldn't want it done to you, don't do it to someone else.
- **Give credit.** If you share someone's art, video, or writing, credit them. It's a small thing that matters a lot to creators.
- **Report harmful content.** You don't have to just scroll past it. Reporting is a low-effort, high-impact action.
- **Remember, there's a person behind every profile.** A comment that takes you two seconds to type can affect someone for days. That works in both directions—negative comments cause real harm, and genuine, kind ones cause real good.

Digital Life Glow Up Tracker

Your digital habits are habits like any other—they can be built, adjusted, and improved over time. This tracker helps you notice what's working, what isn't, and where you're getting smarter about how you show up online.

Week of:

____

POSTING CHECK:

Did I pause before posting anything this week?

☐ Yes ☐ No ☐ Didn't post anything

Was there anything I almost posted but decided against? What stopped me?

____

PRIVACY CHECK:

Did I share anything this week that I wish I hadn't?

☐ Yes ☐ No

If yes, what happened and what would I do differently?

____

COMPARISON CHECK (Digital Edition):

Did scrolling make me feel worse about myself this week?

☐ Yes ☐ No ☐ A little

What account or content was the biggest trigger?

____

RED FLAG CHECK:

Did anything feel "sus" online this week—a weird DM, an account that seemed off, a request that felt uncomfortable?

☐ Yes (did I tell an adult? ☐ Yes ☐ No)

☐ No

DIGITAL WIN THIS WEEK:

One way I showed up well online (positive comment, smart privacy decision, helped someone, didn't engage with drama, etc.):

____

SCREEN TIME REALITY CHECK:

How did my screen time feel this week — balanced, too much, or about right?

☐ Balanced   ☐ Too much   ☐ About right

One small adjustment I want to make next week:

DIGITAL CONFIDENCE CHECK:

How in control of my digital life do I feel this week?

1 ---- 2 ---- 3 ---- 4 ---- 5 ---- 6 ---- 7 ---- 8 ---- 9 ---- 10

Monthly Reflection

- What's one digital habit I've improved this month?

- What account or app has been most positive for me? Most negative?

- Did I check my privacy settings this month? ☐ Yes   ☐ Not yet

- What's one thing I posted this month that I'm genuinely proud of?

- What's one way I want to be a better digital citizen next month?

You Own Your Digital Life

Here's what you now know how to do:

- Pause before you post and run the three-question check

- Handle likes, comments, and the approval loop without letting it run your mood

- Protect your personal information with the Never Share list

- Understand your digital footprint and what it means long-term

- Check and maintain your privacy settings across every platform

- Secure your accounts with strong passwords and two-factor authentication

- Spot catfishing, grooming behavior, and other red flags before they escalate

- Use the Report, Block, Tell framework whenever something feels wrong

- Show up as a positive digital citizen who makes online spaces slightly better

The digital world isn't going anywhere. And you're going to spend a significant portion of your life navigating it. The skills in this chapter aren't just for middle school—they're for life. The sooner you build them, the longer they protect you.

ten

communication hacks—talking to teachers, adults, and classmates

Communication is one of those skills that sounds simple until you actually have to do it in a hard moment. Asking your teacher why you got a bad grade. Telling your parents something happened that you're not sure how to explain. Speaking up in class when you're not totally sure of your answer. Telling a friend something they did hurt your feelings. Advocating for yourself when an adult has the wrong idea about who you are or what happened.

These situations require more than just talking. They require knowing what to say, how to say it, when to say it, and how to handle it when the conversation doesn't go the way you hoped. They require self-advocacy—the ability to speak up for your own needs clearly and respectfully, even when it's uncomfortable.

This is the chapter that ties everything together. Because every other skill in this book—handling drama, managing stress, organizing your schoolwork, standing up to bullying—eventually requires you to communicate with another human being. Let's build that toolkit all the way up.

> "I spent two whole months not understanding something in math because I was too embarrassed to ask. When I finally asked, my teacher spent five minutes explaining it, and everything clicked. Two months of confusion for five minutes of asking. That was a turning point for me."
>
> — Kenji, 7th grade

How to Ask for Help Without Feeling Embarrassed

Let's start here because everything else builds on it: You cannot navigate middle school successfully without asking for help sometimes. Not because you're not smart or capable — but because you're a person in a new environment dealing with harder material, more complex social situations, and more expectations than you've ever had before. Everyone needs help. The students who get the most out of school are the ones who ask for it.

Why It Feels So Hard

Asking for help feels embarrassing for a few overlapping reasons:

- **Fear of judgment.** "If I ask, everyone will know I don't get it." In reality, the people who ask questions in class are usually the ones other students are silently grateful to — because they had the same question and didn't want to ask either.
- **Fear of looking dumb.** Related but distinct: the worry that not understanding something means you're not smart. It doesn't. It means you haven't learned it yet. Those are completely different things.
- **Not wanting to bother anyone.** Teachers, especially, get this. "I don't want to take up their time." But teachers went into teaching because they want to help students learn. Asking them to help you learn is literally what they are there for.
- **Not knowing how to ask.** Sometimes the block isn't emotional — it's that you genuinely don't know how to start the conversation. That's what the scripts below are for.

Scripts for Asking for Help In Person

In class, to a teacher:

"Excuse me — I'm not sure I followed that last part. Could you explain it again?"

"I understand up to [specific point] but I get lost after that. Can you walk me through it?"

"Could you show me another example? I think seeing it again would help."

After class or during office hours:

"Hey, do you have a minute? I've been struggling with [specific topic] and I want to make sure I understand it before the test."

"I got this back and I'm not sure what I did wrong. Could you help me understand what I should have done differently?"

To a classmate:

"Hey, did you understand what she was saying about [topic]? I'm a little lost."

"Your notes are so good—could I compare mine to yours after class? I think I missed something."

Choosing the Right Moment

Even the best question at the wrong moment can backfire. Here's when to approach:

✔ **Good timing:** Before class starts, after class ends, during a work period, during designated office hours, or when the teacher has clearly finished a lesson segment and is circulating

✗ **Bad timing:** Mid-lecture while others are listening, the second before the bell rings, when the teacher is clearly managing something else, or in front of the whole class if your question is personal

How to signal politely that you need a moment:

"When you have a second—" [then wait for them to turn to you]

"Is now a good time to ask something quickly?"

Handling Shyness: The Baby-Step Approach

If asking for help feels genuinely terrifying, build up to it gradually:

Week 1: Ask ONE question per week. Doesn't matter how small. Just one.

Week 2: Ask one question in class and one after class. Still low stakes.

Week 3+: Notice how teachers respond. Most are warm and helpful. Use that evidence to gradually reduce the fear.

The buddy system: If approaching a teacher alone feels impossible, ask a friend to walk with you or stand nearby while you ask. Having someone there reduces the emotional risk enough to make it doable.

"I Don't Get It!"—What to Say When Homework Makes Zero Sense

There's a difference between being frustrated with homework and being genuinely, fundamentally stuck. Knowing which one you're dealing with helps you figure out the right response.

The "Am I Stuck or Just Frustrated?" Checklist

Before you declare the homework impossible, run through this:

☐ **Re-read the instructions slowly.** Sometimes what seems confusing makes sense the second time.

☐ **Look at your class notes.** The answer or a close version of it is often right there.

☐ **Try the first step only.** Don't look at the whole problem at once. Just: what's the very first thing I need to do here?

☐ **Look at a similar example.** From your textbook, notes, or a quick search. Can you follow the pattern?

☐ **Give it ten minutes.** Actual focused minutes, not frustrated staring. Sometimes your brain needs a warm-up period.

If you've done all of that and you're still completely lost—you're stuck, not just frustrated. That's when you reach out.

Scripts for Explaining Exactly What's Confusing

The more specific you can be about where you're lost, the faster someone can help you. Vague doesn't help—specific does:

Vague (harder to help): *"I don't understand the homework."*

Specific (much easier to help): *"I understand steps one and two, but when I get to step three and have to convert the fractions, I lose track of what I'm supposed to do with the denominator."*

More specific scripts:

> *"I'm fine with the first part, but I get completely lost when we get to [specific concept]."*

> *"I've read this three times and I still don't understand what the question is actually asking me to do."*

> *"Can you walk me through just this one step? I think if I see it once I'll be able to do the rest."*

> *"I tried it and got [answer]. I don't understand why that's wrong."*

Using Visuals to Show Where You're Stuck

Sometimes words aren't the best tool. Try these instead:

Mark-up the worksheet: Circle, underline, or put a question mark next to the specific part that confuses you before you bring it to the teacher. Showing is faster than explaining.

Write your question IN the margin: "I don't understand why we multiply here instead of divide." Having it written means you won't forget what you wanted to ask in the moment.

Show your work up to the sticking point: "I got to here—and then I didn't know what to do next." Teachers can immediately see where your thinking went off track.

If the Help Doesn't Help

Sometimes an explanation doesn't click the first time. That's not failure—it's just how learning works. Here's what to do:

"Thank you—I think I need to try it myself and see if it clicks. Can I come back if I'm still confused?"

"I'm still a bit foggy on it. Is there a video or a practice resource you'd recommend?"

"Could you explain the [specific part] one more time? I almost have it."

How to Talk to Teachers About Problems (Even If You're Shy)

Sometimes you need to talk to a teacher about something beyond academics—a seating issue, a problem with a partner, feedback you don't understand, or something happening in the classroom that's affecting you. These conversations feel higher-stakes because they're more personal. But they're often the most important ones to have.

Conversations Beyond "I Don't Understand the Homework"

Seating or classroom environment:

"Hey, I wanted to talk to you privately about something. I've been having trouble focusing where I'm sitting—would it be possible to move?"

"The noise level near me makes it hard for me to concentrate. Is there anything we can do about that?"

Project partner issues:

"I'm having some trouble with my project partnership and I'd like to talk to you about it privately. Do you have a few minutes?"

"The work isn't being split evenly and I'm not sure how to handle it. Can you help me figure out what to do?"

GRADE OR FEEDBACK you don't understand:

"I got my paper back and I want to make sure I understand what I can do better. Can we go over the feedback together?"

"I'm worried about my grade in this class. Can we talk about what I'm missing and what I can do to improve?"

Something personal affecting your schoolwork:

"I've been dealing with something outside of school, and it's been affecting my focus. I don't need to go into detail, but I wanted you to know in case you've noticed a change."

The Full Email Template for Teachers

Chapter 5 covered the basics of emailing about a missing assignment. Here's the full, expanded email template for any kind of teacher communication — from grade questions to personal issues to requests for help:

> **Subject line:** Be specific. "Question about my grade" is better than "Hi." "Project concern — [Your Name], Period [X]" is better than "Something I wanted to ask."

Sample email structure:

Hi Mr./Ms. [Last Name],

I hope you're doing well. I'm writing because [one sentence stating what you want to address].

[Two to three sentences explaining the situation clearly and specifically. Stick to facts. Use "I" statements. Don't blame or accuse.]

[One sentence stating what you're asking for: a meeting, clarification, a second chance, an extension, etc.]

Thank you for your time. I appreciate your help with this.

[Your name], Period [X]

Example — asking about a grade:

Hi Ms. Rivera,

I hope you're doing well. I'm writing because I received my essay grade and I wanted to make sure I understand the feedback so I can do better next time.

I put a lot of work into the assignment and was surprised by the score. I'd love to understand specifically what I could improve on, especially regarding the analysis section.

Would it be possible to meet briefly before or after class this week to go over it together?

Thank you so much for your time.

Jordan Lee, Period 4

Pre-send checklist:

☐ Title + last name in greeting (not first name unless they've said to use it)

☐ Specific and clear—not vague or rambling

☐ No blame, accusations, or emotional language

☐ A specific, reasonable ask

☐ Spellchecked, no texting abbreviations, no ALL CAPS

☐ Your name and class period at the end

What to Do If a Teacher Doesn't Respond

Give it two school days. If you haven't heard back:

1. **Try in person:** "Hi, I sent you an email a couple of days ago—did you get a chance to see it?" Friendly, not accusatory.
2. **Try a different channel:** Some teachers prefer a note left on their desk, or a question via the class platform (Google Classroom, etc.).
3. **Ask the counselor for help:** If you genuinely need to communicate with a teacher and it's not happening, a counselor can often facilitate.

Real Talk with Adults—Getting Support When You Feel Misunderstood

Here's a hard truth: Adults don't always get it right. Not because they don't care—most of them do—but because they're filtering your experience through their own, which is different from yours in some significant ways. They didn't grow up with social media. They don't always understand how group chat dynamics work or how intense middle school social hierarchies feel. And sometimes they're just tired, distracted, or dealing with their own stuff.

That doesn't mean you stop trying to communicate with them. It means you learn how to communicate in ways that are more likely to land.

> "My parents kept saying 'just ignore it' about something that was really bothering me at school. I finally said, 'I know you're trying to help, but that advice isn't working, and I need something different.' My mom actually stopped and said, 'Okay, tell me more.' It was the first time she really listened. I had to tell her HOW to help before she could."
>
> — Aaliyah, 8th grade

Why Adults Sometimes Miss the Mark

Generational gap: They didn't grow up with the internet, smartphones, or the social pressures of middle school in 2026. Some things genuinely don't translate.

Minimizing instinct: Adults who love you sometimes minimize your problems because seeing you hurt is hard for them. "It'll be fine" is often their way of coping with their own worry about you.

Problem-solving mode: Many adults, especially parents, jump immediately to fixing things when what you actually need first is to feel heard. They skip the listening and go straight to solutions.

Different risk thresholds: What feels enormous to you might feel small to someone with decades of perspective. This doesn't make your feeling wrong—it just means you might need to explain the stakes more specifically.

They're human: They're tired, stressed, and imperfect. Sometimes the timing is just bad. That's worth knowing without it meaning they don't care.

Scripts for Getting Adults to Actually Listen

When you need them to listen before they fix:

"I need to tell you about something that's been bothering me. I'm not asking you to fix it right now—I just need you to hear me first."

"It's hard to explain, but can you listen without giving advice yet? I'll let you know when I'm ready for that part."

When they're minimizing or dismissing what you're feeling:

"I know it might seem small, but it feels really big to me right now. Can you help me work through it even if it doesn't seem like a huge deal?"

"I hear you saying it'll be fine—but right now I'm not fine, and I could use some support getting there."

When they have the wrong idea about what happened:

"I think there might be a misunderstanding about what actually happened. Can I explain my side?"

"What you heard isn't quite what happened. Here's what I experienced: [specific, calm explanation]."

When you need something specific from them:

"What I actually need right now is [specific thing]—not advice, just [someone to listen / a hug / help emailing the teacher / some space]."

"I know you want to help. The most helpful thing right now would be [specific action]."

When the Conversation Gets Heated

Sometimes these conversations go sideways. Your emotions spike. Their emotions spike. It stops being productive. Here's how to handle that:

If you feel yourself getting too upset to communicate clearly:

"I want to keep talking about this but I need a few minutes to calm down first. Can we come back to it in ten minutes?"

If they're getting too upset or the conversation is escalating:

"I don't think either of us is being heard right now. Can we take a break and come back to this?"

If you feel shut down or dismissed:

"I feel like I'm not being heard. I'm not trying to be difficult—I genuinely need help with this. Can we try again?"

Pausing isn't giving up. It's a strategy. Conversations that happen when everyone is calm almost always go better than ones that happen in the heat of the moment.

Finding the Right Adult When the Obvious One Isn't Working

Not every important conversation has to happen with a parent. Not every school concern has to go to your homeroom teacher. Part of self-advocacy is knowing the full landscape of support available to you and choosing strategically.

At school:

At school:

- School counselor (for academic, social, and emotional issues—this is their job)
- A teacher you trust who isn't directly involved in the issue
- Assistant principal or principal (for serious school-level issues)
- School psychologist, if available
- A coach or club advisor who knows you well

AT HOME and in your community:

• An aunt, uncle, grandparent, or family friend who has shown they listen well

• An older sibling or cousin who's been through something similar

• A neighbor, youth pastor, or community leader you trust

• A therapist or counselor (your parents can help set this up; it's confidential)

Key trait to look for in any adult ally: They listen more than they talk. They take you seriously. They don't immediately tell your business to everyone. They follow through. If someone has these qualities, they're worth going to.

Talking to Your Peers: The Communication Skills That Actually Matter

This book has given you scripts for talking to teachers and adults. But some of the hardest conversations in middle school are with your peers—telling a friend they hurt you, disagreeing with someone without it becoming a fight, saying no without it becoming a whole thing, and speaking up for yourself in social situations where you feel pressure to stay quiet.

Using "I" Statements (Without Sounding Like a Therapy Script)

"I" statements are a communication technique where you describe your experience without blaming the other person. They sound corny in theory but genuinely work in practice because they're harder to argue with than accusatory statements.

Accusatory (easy to argue with): *"You always leave me out of things."*

I-statement (harder to argue with): *"I've been feeling left out lately, and I wanted to talk about it."*

Accusatory: *"You told everyone my secret."*

I-statement: *"I found out something I told you in private got shared, and it really hurt me. I need to understand what happened."*

The formula: *"I feel [emotion] when [specific situation] because [why it matters to me]. What I need is [specific ask]."*

Saying No Without a Full Explanation

Middle school creates a lot of pressure to go along with things—to say yes to plans you don't want to go to, to agree with opinions you don't hold, to do things that make you uncomfortable because everyone else is doing them. Learning to say no clearly and calmly—without an elaborate excuse or apology—is one of the most useful things you can do for yourself.

Scripts for saying no cleanly:

> *"No, I'm good. Thanks, though."*

> *"That's not really my thing."*

> *"I'm going to sit this one out."*

> *"I'm not comfortable with that."*

You don't owe anyone a detailed explanation for declining something that doesn't work for you. "I don't want to" is a complete reason. The more elaborate the excuse, the more it invites pushback.

Disagreeing Without It Becoming a Fight

You're going to disagree with people. That's part of having your own opinions, which is actually a sign of a healthy developing identity. The goal isn't to avoid disagreement—it's to disagree in a way that respects both people and doesn't blow up the relationship.

Scripts for disagreeing respectfully:

> *"I see it differently—can I tell you why?"*

> *"I hear you, but I don't agree with that part. Here's my thinking."*

> *"We might just see this differently, and that's okay."*

> *"I'm not sure I agree, but I want to think about what you said."*

What to do when someone won't let the disagreement go:

> *"I think we're going to see this differently, and I'm okay with that." [Change subject]*

"I've heard your point. I'm not going to change my mind right now, and I'd rather just move on."

Delivering Hard News or Feedback to a Friend

Telling a friend something they don't want to hear—that they hurt you, that they're acting differently, that something they did had consequences—is genuinely difficult. Here's a framework that makes it easier:

Start with care. *"I'm telling you this because I actually care about our friendship."* This signals your intent before the content.

Be specific, not general. *"When you [specific action], I felt [specific feeling]."* Not: "You've been a bad friend lately."

Say what you need. *"What I'd need going forward is [specific thing]."*

Give them space to respond. Ask: "How are you feeling about what I just said?" Then actually listen.

Resolving Misunderstandings Before They Become Drama

A lot of middle school conflict is actually miscommunication—something was said that was taken differently than intended, or something was assumed that wasn't true. Before a misunderstanding escalates, try this:

"Hey, I want to check something with you directly before I assume the worst. Did you mean [X] when you said [Y]?"

"Something happened that I'm confused about. Can I ask you about it directly?"

"I heard something, and I want to hear your side before I decide how to feel about it."

Going to the source directly—before going to mutual friends, before posting, before assuming—resolves about 80% of middle school misunderstandings before they ever become full-blown drama. It's one of the most underused communication moves there is.

> "I almost lost my best friend because I assumed she was mad at me based on how she was acting. Turned out she was having a terrible week at home and it had nothing to do with me at all. I almost started a whole thing over nothing. I ask now instead of assuming."
>
> — Brianna, 7th grade

Communication Glow Up Tracker

Communication is a skill, which means it gets better with practice and intentional reflection. This tracker helps you notice where you're growing and where you still want to improve.

Week of:

____

HELP-ASKING CHECK:

Did I ask for help with something this week (academic or personal)?

☐ Yes ☐ No

If yes, how did it go?

____

If no, what held me back?

____

HARD CONVERSATION CHECK:

Was there a conversation I needed to have but avoided this week?

☐ Yes — What was it, and what stopped me?

____

☐ No

Did I have a hard conversation that went well?

____

ADULT COMMUNICATION CHECK:

Did I communicate with a teacher or adult about something this week?

☐ Yes ☐ No

What worked? What would I do differently?

____

____

PEER COMMUNICATION WIN:

One moment this week where I communicated clearly, honestly, or bravely with a peer:

____

SOMETHING I WANT TO SAY (but haven't yet):

Write it here. Practice the words. Plan when and how you'll say it.

COMMUNICATION CONFIDENCE CHECK:

How confident do I feel communicating my needs this week?

1 ---- 2 ---- 3 ---- 4 ---- 5 ---- 6 ---- 7 ---- 8 ---- 9 ---- 10

Monthly Reflection

- What's one conversation I had this month that I'm proud of?

- What's one conversation I avoided that I want to have next month?

- Which communication skill has improved the most since I started paying attention?

- Which adult in my life do I communicate with most easily? What makes it work?

- What's one communication habit I want to build next month?

Your Voice Matters — Use It

Here's what you now know how to do:

- Ask for help without shame — and choose the right moment to do it

- Explain exactly where you're confused so people can actually help you

- Talk to teachers about issues beyond academics — seating, grades, partners, personal situations

- Write emails that are clear, professional, and get results

- Get adults to actually listen by telling them what kind of support you need

- Correct misunderstandings and hold your ground when someone has the wrong idea

- Find the right adult ally when the obvious one isn't working

- Use I-statements to address peer conflict without starting a war

- Say no clearly and without a fifteen-minute explanation

• Disagree respectfully, deliver hard feedback with care, and resolve misunderstandings before they spiral

Self-advocacy—the ability to clearly and respectfully communicate your needs—is one of the highest-value skills you can build in middle school. It will serve you in high school, in college, in jobs, in relationships, and in every difficult situation you'll ever face. The earlier you start building it, the better.

healthy habits for body and brain

Everything else in this book—managing drama, handling stress, building confidence, communicating clearly, staying organized—works better when your body and brain have what they need. And it works significantly worse when they don't.

This isn't a wellness lecture. It's not about being perfect or following some rigid routine. It's about understanding the connection between how you treat your body and how you feel, think, focus, and cope. Because middle school is demanding—socially, academically, emotionally—and the foundation you build right now matters more than most people realize.

Four things. That's all this chapter is about: sleep, food, movement, and screen time. Not perfectly. Just intentionally.

Sleep: The Superpower You're Probably Skipping

Let's start with the one that makes the biggest difference and gets the least respect: sleep. Middle schoolers need 8–9 hours of sleep per night. Most get significantly less—often six or fewer. And the gap between what your brain needs and what it's getting doesn't just make you tired. It makes everything harder.

What Sleep Actually Does (It's Not Just Rest)

While you sleep, your brain is not offline. It's doing some of its most important work:

• **Memory consolidation:** Everything you learned during the day—in class, from practice, from experience—gets processed and stored during sleep.

Pulling an all-nighter before a test actively works against you. The studying you did the night before consolidates while you sleep.

• **Emotional regulation:** The part of your brain responsible for managing big feelings (remember Chapter 7?) resets during sleep. When you're underslept, your emotional responses are more intense, less controlled, and harder to bring back down.

• **Physical repair:** Hormones responsible for growth and tissue repair are released primarily during deep sleep. If you're going through puberty right now, your body literally needs this time.

• **Immune function:** Chronic sleep deprivation weakens your immune system. If you seem to get sick more often than others, sleep is worth examining.

• **Decision-making and focus:** Your prefrontal cortex—the rational decision-making center of your brain—is especially sensitive to sleep deprivation. Tired = worse judgment, slower reaction time, harder time concentrating.

> "Every hour of sleep is worth about two hours of studying. That's not an exact number, but it's the vibe. I used to stay up until 1 AM cramming and wonder why I couldn't remember anything during the test."
>
> — Terrell, 8th grade

Why Middle Schoolers Are Chronically Underslept: The Real Reasons

• **Delayed sleep phase:** During puberty, your body's internal clock shifts later. You genuinely don't feel tired until later at night—this is biological, not laziness. But school still starts early, creating a structural mismatch that affects almost every middle and high schooler.

• **Screens at night:** The blue light emitted by phones, tablets, and laptops suppresses melatonin—the hormone that signals your brain it's time to sleep. Scrolling at 10 PM is essentially telling your brain it's noon.

• **Homework and activities:** Real-time pressures. Late practice, heavy homework loads, and after-school jobs. These are legitimate.

• **Social FOMO:** Staying up because the group chat is active, because you don't want to miss something, because being online feels more interesting than sleeping. This one is worth being honest with yourself about.

• **Anxiety:** Racing thoughts at bedtime. Worry about tomorrow. Replaying today. If anxiety is keeping you up, Chapter 7's techniques apply here too — and it's worth talking to someone about it.

Building a Sleep Routine That Actually Works

You don't need a perfect routine. You need a consistent one. Your body clock responds to regularity far more than to any single hack.

The 30-minute wind-down:

1. Screens off or on Night Shift/warm filter 30 minutes before bed. Not five minutes — thirty. This is the single most impactful sleep change most people can make.

2. Do something calm. Reading (a physical book or e-reader without blue light), light stretching, journaling, and listening to calm music. Something that signals to your brain: we're transitioning to sleep mode.

3. Keep your room cool and dark. Your body temperature drops during sleep. A cooler room (around 65–68°F) helps you fall asleep faster. Blackout curtains or a sleep mask block light that interrupts deep sleep.

4. Same bedtime on school nights. Even 15 minutes of consistency helps your body clock. Pick a time and try to stick to it within 30 minutes every night.

If you can't fall asleep:

• 4-7-8 breathing: in for 4, hold for 7, out for 8. Repeat three times.

• Progressive muscle relaxation: tense each muscle group for five seconds, release. Start with your feet, work up to your face.

• Write your worries down. If racing thoughts are the problem, getting them out of your head and onto paper gives your brain permission to let them go for now.

• Don't look at the clock. Clock-watching increases anxiety about not sleeping, which makes it harder to sleep.

The weekend sleep trap:

Sleeping until noon on weekends feels restorative, but actually makes Monday morning worse by shifting your body clock even further. Try to stay within an hour of your weekday wake time on weekends — or at most two hours. It's one of the most effective things you can do for Monday-morning focus.

One-week experiment: Phone out of your room for seven nights. Not across the room—out of the room. Track how your sleep and mood change. Most people are genuinely surprised by the difference.

The Sleep–Mood–Focus Connection in Action

Here's a pattern worth recognizing in your own life:

Poor sleep → lower frustration tolerance → more conflict with friends and family → more stress → harder to fall asleep → more poor sleep.

Good sleep → better emotional regulation → clearer thinking → better performance → lower stress → easier to sleep.

The loop runs in both directions. Fixing sleep doesn't fix everything, but it makes everything else more fixable.

Fueling Your Brain—Food, Hydration, and Energy Without the Crash

Your brain is an organ. It needs fuel. And the fuel you give it—or don't give it—directly affects how well it functions. This isn't about dieting, about eating perfectly, or about following rules. It's about understanding the connection between what you eat and how you feel, so you can make choices that actually support you.

Important: This section is about general nutrition for energy and brain function—not about weight, body shape, or appearance. If you're struggling with your relationship with food in any way, talking to a trusted adult or doctor is the right move. The National Alliance for Eating Disorders helpline (1-866-662-1235) is also available if you need it.

The Breakfast Question

Research is consistent: students who eat breakfast have better concentration, memory, and problem-solving ability than those who don't. Your brain runs primarily on glucose, and after 8–9 hours of sleep without food, those stores are depleted. Trying to focus in the first period without breakfast is like trying to drive a car with an empty tank.

The reality: You might not be hungry in the morning. That's common, especially if you ate late the night before or you're naturally not a morning person. You don't have to eat a big breakfast—something small is better than nothing.

Quick, low-effort breakfast options that actually work:

• A banana and a handful of nuts (takes 30 seconds)

- Greek yogurt with granola (kept in the fridge, ready to grab)

- Peanut butter on whole grain toast (two minutes)

- A boiled egg prepped the night before

- A smoothie with fruit, milk or yogurt, and nut butter if you have a blender and a few extra minutes

- Even just a glass of milk and a piece of fruit is meaningfully better than nothing

If you consistently have no appetite in the morning, try eating a lighter dinner or earlier in the evening. Your morning appetite is often affected by when you ate the night before.

The Energy Crash: Why It Happens and How to Avoid It

The energy crash—that foggy, can't-focus feeling that hits in the middle of the afternoon—is usually caused by a spike and drop in blood sugar. It happens when you eat something high in simple sugar (a candy bar, a soda, most energy drinks, sugary cereals) that causes a rapid rise in blood sugar followed by an equally rapid drop.

Foods that cause crashes:

✗ Sugary drinks (soda, energy drinks, sweetened coffee)

✗ Candy and heavily processed sweets

✗ White bread, white rice, most packaged snack foods

✗ Most vending machine options

Foods that provide sustained energy:

✓ **Complex carbs:** Whole grain bread, oats, brown rice, fruit—these digest slowly and provide a steady supply of glucose rather than a spike

✓ **Protein:** Eggs, nuts, beans, cheese, meat, Greek yogurt—keeps you full longer and stabilizes blood sugar

✓ **Healthy fats:** Avocado, nuts, olive oil—brain tissue is largely made of fat; these support cognitive function

✓ **Water:** Dehydration causes fatigue and difficulty concentrating before you even feel thirsty

Hydration: The Underrated Brain Hack

Your brain is about 75% water. Even mild dehydration—1–2% below optimal—measurably impairs focus, memory, and mood. And you can be mildly dehydrated without feeling thirsty. Thirst is a late signal, not an early one.

How to actually drink more water without making it a whole thing:

1. Keep a water bottle at your desk and refill it once between each class
2. Drink a full glass of water first thing in the morning before anything else
3. If you hate plain water, add fruit, cucumber, or a small splash of juice
4. Eat water-rich foods: most fruits and vegetables count toward hydration
5. Check your urine color—pale yellow means well-hydrated, dark yellow means drink more

What about caffeine?

Coffee, energy drinks, and heavily caffeinated teas are not recommended for middle schoolers—your nervous system is still developing, and caffeine affects it more strongly than it affects adults. Caffeine also disrupts sleep, which you already know is critical. If you're relying on caffeine to get through the day, the underlying problem is probably sleep deprivation, not a caffeine deficiency.

School Lunch Survival: Getting What You Need in 25 Minutes

School lunch is not always ideal. The options might be limited, the time is short, and social dynamics can make it hard to focus on actually eating. A few realistic strategies:

Eat something. Even if the options aren't great, eating something is better than nothing. An empty stomach heading into afternoon classes makes everything harder.

Pack something small if you can. A piece of fruit, a granola bar, or a small bag of nuts you keep in your bag gives you a backup option and a buffer for midday snacks.

Protein first. If you're choosing between pizza and grilled chicken, the protein will keep you focused longer throughout the afternoon.

Sit down and actually eat. It sounds obvious, but rushing through lunch while managing social chaos means you don't eat enough, and you don't absorb it as well. Even five minutes of focused eating is better than fifteen minutes of distracted nibbling.

"I started bringing an apple and some almonds in my bag because lunch at school never kept me full. The energy difference in afternoon classes was actually noticeable. I stopped feeling like I was going to fall asleep in history."

— Simone, 7th grade

Movement: Your Brain's Best Friend

You've heard this before: exercise is good for you. What you might not fully appreciate is how directly and immediately physical movement affects your brain—not just your body. This isn't about fitness goals or athletic performance. It's about using movement as a tool for clearer thinking, a better mood, and lower stress.

What Happens in Your Brain When You Move

Endorphins release: Natural mood-boosters that reduce pain and create a mild sense of well-being. The "runner's high" is real, but you don't have to run—any sustained movement triggers it.

Cortisol drops: Cortisol is your primary stress hormone. Exercise is one of the most effective ways to lower it. This is why a 10-minute walk after a stressful day makes such a noticeable difference.

BDNF increases: Brain-Derived Neurotrophic Factor is sometimes called "Miracle-Gro for the brain." It supports the growth of new brain cells and strengthens neural connections—including the ones involved in learning and memory. Exercise is one of the best ways to trigger its release.

Focus improves: Studies consistently show that even a short bout of moderate exercise improves concentration and attention for several hours afterward. Moving before doing homework is actually a better strategy than sitting down immediately.

Finding Movement You Don't Hate

The best exercise is the kind you'll actually do. Not the kind you think you should do. If running makes you miserable, don't run. The goal is to find something that gets your heart rate up and that you can sustain. Here's a broad menu to explore:

Team sports and organized activities:

- School sports (basketball, soccer, track, volleyball, swimming, etc.)
- Recreational leagues through parks and community centers
- Club sports or intramural teams

Solo movement that doesn't feel like "exercise":

- Dancing — in your room, alone, with music that makes you want to move
- Skateboarding, biking, or rollerblading
- YouTube workout videos (there are thousands — 10-minute options, no equipment needed)
- Walking with a podcast or playlist
- Shooting hoops, playing catch, kicking a ball around
- Rock climbing at an indoor gym
- Martial arts, dance classes, yoga

Stealth movement (built into your day without carving out extra time):

- Walk or bike to school if possible
- Take the stairs intentionally and with purpose
- Do homework standing up or pacing for at least part of it
- Stretch for five minutes between classes or homework sessions
- Walk during phone calls instead of sitting

The "10-Minute Reset" Rule

You don't need a 45-minute workout to get the brain benefits of movement. Ten minutes of moderate activity — enough to raise your heart rate and make you slightly breathless — produces measurable improvements in mood and focus. This is your go-to when:

1. You're stressed and can't focus on homework
2. You've been sitting at a screen for more than 90 minutes
3. You're in a bad mood and don't know why
4. You have a test tomorrow, and you're feeling anxious
5. You just had a hard social interaction and need to reset

What counts as a 10-minute reset: a fast walk around the block, jumping jacks and push-ups until you're slightly out of breath, dancing to two or three songs, a quick bike ride, or any movement that gets your body going.

Movement and Mental Health

Physical activity has been shown in clinical research to be as effective as medication for mild to moderate depression and anxiety in some cases, and it has essentially no negative side effects. This doesn't mean it replaces professional treatment when that's needed. But it does mean that if you're feeling low, anxious, or emotionally flat, moving your body is one of the highest-return actions available to you.

Not because it fixes the problem. Because it gives your brain the chemistry it needs to cope with the problem.

> "I was going through a really hard time socially and I started going for a run every day after school. Not to get fit—just because I needed to do something with the feeling. It didn't make the situation go away but I could think about it more clearly after. It became the thing I counted on."
>
> — Mia, 8th grade

Screen Time Balance—Using Technology Without Letting It Use You

Screens are not the enemy. Your phone, your laptop, your gaming console—these are tools. They connect you with people you care about, help you learn, give you creative outlets, and provide genuine entertainment and rest. The problem isn't screens. The problem is unintentional screen use—time that wasn't really chosen, picked up because picking up the phone was the path of least resistance, and left you feeling worse instead of better.

The goal of this section is not to use less technology. It's to use it with more intention so it actually serves you rather than draining you.

The Screen Time Reality Check

Most people underestimate their daily screen time by 30–50%. Here's how to find out where yours actually is:

iPhone: Settings → Screen Time. Shows daily and weekly breakdowns by app category.

Android: Settings → Digital Wellbeing & Parental Controls. Same information.

What to look for: Total daily average, time on social vs. productive apps, number of times you picked up your phone, and which apps are getting the most time.

When you see the actual number, you'll have information you can work with. Most people find at least one or two categories that genuinely surprise them.

Not All Screen Time Is Equal

A blanket rule of "less screen time is better" misses something important: context. Two hours of video chatting with a close friend is very different from two hours of passive scrolling. Here's a more useful framework:

✅ **ACTIVE USE:** (generally okay and often good):

- Creating content: writing, drawing, making videos, coding, music production
- Learning: tutorials, educational videos, research
- Communicating with real people you care about: video calls, meaningful conversations
- Playing games with real social elements and intentional engagement

⚠️ **PASSIVE USE (fine in moderation, problematic in excess):**

- Watching YouTube or streaming (can be relaxing and valuable— just time-box it)
- Scrolling social media feeds without a specific purpose
- Background TV while doing other things

⚫ **DRAINING USE (worth limiting):**

- Passive scrolling that makes you feel worse about yourself or your life
- Doomscrolling news or content that raises your anxiety without giving you anything useful
- Using screens as emotional avoidance (reaching for the phone every time you feel bored, uncomfortable, or sad)
- Late-night use that reliably cuts into sleep

Practical Screen Boundaries That Don't Feel Like Punishment

The phone-free zones:

Bedroom at night: Charge your phone in another room. This one change— more than any other—improves both sleep and morning mood for most people who try it.

Mealtimes: Phone down during meals, even when you're eating alone. Give your brain a break from stimulus.

First 30 minutes after school: Before you open any app, take 30 minutes to decompress, eat something, or go outside. This transition time reduces the anxious urge to check your notifications immediately.

First 10 minutes of the morning: Don't check your phone the moment you wake up. Give yourself a few minutes to be in your own head before the outside world comes in.

APP LIMITS AND TIMERS:

1. Set daily limits on specific apps through Screen Time (iPhone) or Digital Wellbeing (Android)
2. Use the "Downtime" feature to automatically lock apps during homework hours or after a certain time at night
3. Turn off social media push notifications—you check when you want to, not every time something happens

The "intentional pick-up" habit:

Before you pick up your phone, pause for one second and ask: "Why am I picking this up?" If you have a specific reason—checking a message, looking something up, calling someone—great. If the answer is "I don't know," "Just to check," or "Because I'm bored," pause. Decide intentionally whether that's how you want to spend the next however many minutes.

This one small habit—just asking why before picking it up—significantly reduces mindless use for most people who practice it.

> "I put my phone in my backpack when I start homework. Not on my desk. Not in my room. In my backpack. The number of times I checked it went from like every five minutes to basically zero. My homework started taking half as long."
>
> — Dominic, 7th grade

Gaming: Healthy Hobby vs. Avoidance Behavior

Gaming gets a complicated reputation. Here's a more nuanced take:

Gaming can be genuinely good:

→ Problem-solving and strategy games build real cognitive skills

→ Online gaming with friends maintains social connections

→ Creative games (Minecraft, Roblox game creation) support real creative development

→ Gaming as a wind-down and entertainment is a legitimate form of rest

Gaming becomes a problem when:

→ It's the primary way you cope with every difficult emotion

→ You can't stop when you planned to stop, repeatedly

→ It's consistently displacing sleep, homework, and in-person relationships

→ You feel more irritable, anxious, or down when you're not playing

→ You're hiding how much time you spend on it

If gaming is starting to feel compulsive rather than fun, that's worth talking to someone about. It's not a moral failing—it's a signal that something else might need attention.

Building Your Personal Health Baseline

The four habits in this chapter—sleep, food, movement, and intentional screen use—are your foundation. Everything else in this book works better when these are in reasonable shape. They don't have to be perfect. They just have to be present.

Here's a realistic self-assessment:

Your Honest Health Snapshot

SLEEP:

Average hours per night this week: _______

Quality (1–10—how rested do I feel?): ______

Biggest sleep disruptor: ☐ Phone ☐ Anxiety/racing thoughts

☐ Homework ☐ Late activities ☐ Other: _______

One change I could make:

____

FOOD:

Do I eat breakfast most days? ☐ Yes ☐ No ☐ Sometimes

Do I get hungry or crash in the afternoon? ☐ Yes ☐ No ☐ Sometimes

Do I drink enough water? ☐ Yes ☐ No ☐ Trying to

One food habit I want to build:

____

MOVEMENT:

Days per week I move my body intentionally: ______

Activity I actually enjoy:

____

Activity I want to try:

____

Could I fit a 10-minute reset into my day?

☐ Yes ☐ Maybe ☐ When?: ______

SCREEN TIME:

Average daily screen time (check your phone settings): _______

App that takes up the most time: _______

Does this feel intentional or habitual? ☐ Mostly intentional ☐ Mostly habitual ☐ Mix

One boundary I want to set:

The One-Thing Challenge

Don't try to overhaul everything at once. Pick ONE habit from the four areas above that would make the biggest difference in how you feel right now. Just one. Do it consistently for two weeks. Then reassess.

My one thing for the next two weeks:

Why this one? What do I expect to notice if I stick to it?

Check-in date (two weeks from now):

Pro tip: Tell one person about your one thing. Not for accountability pressure — just because saying it out loud makes it more real. Text a friend, tell a parent, or write it in your Glow Up Journal.

Healthy Habits Glow Up Tracker

Your physical health isn't separate from your mental health, your social life, or your academic performance. It's the foundation. This tracker helps you notice the connection between how you take care of your body and how everything else feels.

Week of:

____

SLEEP LOG:

Mon: __ hours **Tue:** __ hours **Wed:** __ hours **Thu:** __ hours **Fri:** __ hours

Weekly average: ____   Phone out of room at night?

☐ Most nights ☐ Some nights ☐ Not yet

FOOD CHECK:

Ate breakfast: Mon ☐ Tue ☐ Wed ☐ Thu ☐ Fri ☐

Drank enough water most days? ☐ Yes ☐ Getting there ☐ Not really

Afternoon energy crash this week? ☐ Yes ☐ No ☐ Once or twice

MOVEMENT LOG:

Days I moved intentionally: _______

What I did:

____

Did I use a 10-minute reset at any point? ☐ Yes ☐ No

SCREEN TIME CHECK:

Daily average this week: _______

Did I pick up my phone intentionally most of the time? ☐ Yes ☐ Mostly ☐ Not really

Did phone use affect my sleep this week? ☐ Yes ☐ No ☐ Probably

BODY–BRAIN CONNECTION:

On the days I slept well, I noticed:

____

On the days I moved my body, I noticed:

____

This week my energy level was (1–10):

____

ONE HEALTH WIN THIS WEEK:

____

HEALTH FOUNDATION CHECK:

How well am I taking care of my body and brain this week?

1 ---- 2 ---- 3 ---- 4 ---- 5 ---- 6 ---- 7 ---- 8 ---- 9 ---- 10

Monthly Reflection

• Which of the four areas (sleep, food, movement, screen time) improved the most this month?

• What's one body–brain connection I've noticed in my own life?

• What's the one health habit that's made the biggest difference to how I feel?

• What's one area I want to focus on next month?

• How has my energy and mood changed since I started paying attention to these four things?

Your Body Is Working For You — Work With It

Here's what you now know:

• What sleep actually does for your brain and why middle schoolers need more of it

• How to build a wind-down routine and what to do when you can't fall asleep

• The connection between food, blood sugar, and afternoon focus

• Quick, realistic breakfast options and how to fuel smarter through the day

• Why movement is a brain tool, not just a fitness tool — and the 10-minute reset

• How to assess your screen time honestly and use technology with intention

• The difference between active, passive, and draining screen use

• Your personal health baseline and the one-thing challenge

You don't have to be perfect at any of this. You just have to be intentional. One good habit, practiced consistently, creates a ripple effect on everything else. Sleep a little better and your mood improves. Move a little more and your stress drops. Eat a little more intentionally and your afternoon focus sharpens. It compounds.

growth mindset and goal setting— building the version of you that you actually want to become

You've made it to the last chapter. And before we get into goal setting and growth mindset, here's something worth saying out loud: The fact that you've read this far—that you picked up this book and kept going—already tells you something important about yourself. You're someone who takes their own development seriously. That's not nothing. That's actually quite a lot.

This chapter is about the mindset that makes everything else in this book work over time. Not just surviving middle school—but using it. Using the hard moments, the failures, the awkward phases, and the slow progress as the raw material for becoming someone you're genuinely proud to be.

Growth mindset. Goal setting. Bouncing back. Celebrating small wins. The Glow Up Yearbook. Let's do this.

Fixed vs. Growth Mindset—Why "I'm Just Not Good At This" Is a Trap

In the 1990s, psychologist Carol Dweck began researching why some students bounce back from failure, and others don't. What she found changed how educators and psychologists think about learning and achievement. The difference wasn't ability. It was a belief.

Specifically: what students believed about whether ability was fixed or changeable.

THERE ARE TWO MINDSETS.

The Fixed Mindset says:

✖ Intelligence and talent are things you either have or you don't

✖ If you're not good at something quickly, you're probably just not built for it

✖ Effort is for people who aren't naturally talented

✖ Failure means you're not smart or capable

✖ Challenges are threats—if you struggle, it reveals your limitations

The Growth Mindset says:

☑ Ability is developed through effort, strategy, and help from others

☑ If you're not good at something yet, that's just where you are right now

☑ Effort is how you get better—it's not a consolation prize

☑ Failure is information, not a verdict

☑ Challenges are opportunities—struggling means you're at the edge of what you currently know

The keyword in the growth mindset is one that gets added to almost everything: yet.

"I'm not good at math." → *"I'm not good at math yet."*

"I can't do this." → *"I can't do this yet."*

"I'll never be like that." → *"I'm not there yet."*

That one word changes your relationship with where you are right now. It keeps the door open.

Fixed Mindset Thoughts in Real Middle School Life

Fixed mindset doesn't always sound like a philosophy. It sounds like this:

- *"I'm just not a math person."*

- *"I've never been a good writer."*

- *"Some people are just naturally confident. I'm not one of them."*

- *"I'm bad at making friends."*

- *"I'm just not athletic."*

- *"I could never do something like that."*

- *"I'm the kind of person who…"* *(usually followed by a limitation)*

These statements feel like self-awareness. They're often actually self-imposed ceilings. The brain takes them as instructions: "Oh, this is who we are. Don't bother trying in this area." And then it stops looking for evidence that contradicts them.

How to Catch and Flip Fixed Mindset Thoughts

You can't just tell yourself to "have a growth mindset." It's a practice, not a switch. Here's how to actually do it:

1. Notice the fixed thought. *"I'm so bad at presentations."* Catch it.

2. Add "yet." *"I'm not good at presentations yet."* Feel the difference.

3. Find the evidence that it's changeable. "Actually, I've gotten less shaky each time. I used to read off the paper 100% of the time. Last time I looked up a few times."

4. Identify the next step. "What's one thing I can do to get slightly better at this? Practice out loud more. Ask my teacher for feedback. Watch someone good at it."

The growth mindset mantra: *"I'm not there yet—and I'm moving in that direction."* Say it. Mean it. Act on it.

Growth Mindset in Action: Real Examples from This Book

Look back at everything you've learned in the past eleven chapters. Every single skill was a growth mindset skill in disguise:

- **Recovering from embarrassing moments (Ch. 6):** "I'm not yet someone who bounces back smoothly—but I'm getting better each time."

- **Managing anxiety (Ch. 7):** "I'm not yet great at calming myself down quickly—but I have tools now, and I'm using them."

- **Communicating with adults (Ch. 10):** "I'm not yet totally comfortable advocating for myself—but I know what to say, and I'm practicing."

- **Asking for help (Ch. 10):** "I'm not yet someone who asks without embarrassment—but I'm doing it anyway."

- **Building healthy habits (Ch. 11):** "I'm not yet consistent with sleep and movement—but I know why it matters, and I'm paying attention."

Middle school is, in many ways, an enormous growth-mindset laboratory. You are surrounded by evidence that you can get better at hard things. You just have to pay attention to it.

> "My sixth-grade math teacher told me I was just not a math person. I believed him for two whole years. Then I got a new teacher in eighth grade who kept saying 'not yet.' I ended up taking advanced math in high school. The difference was literally just believing it was possible."
>
> — Aaliyah, 10th grade

How to Actually Set Goals (Not the Kind You Forget in Three Days)

Goal setting has a reputation problem. Most people have tried it—written goals on New Year's Day, made a list at the start of a school year, filled out a worksheet in advisory, and found that by week two, the goals have evaporated. Not because goals don't work. Most goals are set in a way that makes them almost impossible to stick to.

Here's what actually works.

The Problem with Vague Goals

Vague goal: *"I want to get better grades."*

What's wrong with this: "Better" isn't measurable. "Grades" in general isn't specific. There's no deadline. There's no plan. There's no way to know if you're making progress.

Vague goal: *"I want to be more confident."*

What's wrong with this: Confidence in what context? By when? What would "more confident" actually look like in your life? How would you know you got there?

Vague goals feel inspiring for about 48 hours and then fade because your brain can't act on them. You need something specific enough that you know exactly what to do tomorrow.

SMART Goals: The Framework That Actually Works

A SMART goal is:

• **S — Specific:** Exactly what do you want to accomplish? In which subject, skill, or area of your life?

• **M — Measurable:** How will you know when you've achieved it? What's the number, frequency, or observable sign?

• **A — Achievable:** Is this realistically possible given your current situation? Stretch goals are good—impossible goals just lead to giving up.

• **R — Relevant:** Does this matter to you? Not to your parents, your teacher, or your friend—to you. Goals you actually care about stick.

• **T — Time-bound:** By when? A deadline creates urgency and makes the goal feel real.

Vague goal transformed into SMART goal:

Vague: *"I want to get better grades."*

SMART: *"I want to raise my science grade from a C to a B by the end of the semester by reviewing my notes for 15 minutes every Sunday, asking for help when I'm confused instead of waiting, and turning in all assignments on time."*

Vague: *"I want to be less anxious about presentations."*

SMART: *"By the end of this school year, I want to give three presentations without reading directly off my notes the whole time. I'll practice out loud at home the night before each one and use the box breathing technique before I go up."*

The Three Types of Goals Worth Setting in Middle School

1. Academic goals

Tied to specific subjects, assignments, or study habits. These are the most straightforward to measure.

Examples: Improve my essay grade by focusing on topic sentences. Study two days before tests instead of the night before. Turn in every assignment for one full marking period.

2. Personal growth goals

About who you're becoming—habits, character, mindset. Harder to measure but often more meaningful.

Examples: Ask for help once a week instead of staying confused. Do something uncomfortable once a week to build confidence. Say something kind to at least one person every day.

3. Interest and skill goals

About getting better at something you care about—a sport, instrument, art form, craft, or hobby. These goals are intrinsically motivating because they're about something you genuinely love.

Examples: Practice guitar for 20 minutes four times a week. Read one book per month in a genre I haven't tried. Learn to cook three new recipes by the end of the year.

Setting Your Goals Right Now

Use the SMART framework to set one goal in each category. Start with just one per type. Trying to set ten goals at once is how you end up keeping zero.

MY ACADEMIC GOAL:

I want to: ____

By when: ____

My specific plan (what I will do, how often): _______________________________

____

How I'll know I've achieved it: _______________________________

MY PERSONAL GROWTH GOAL:

I want to: ____

By when: ____

My specific plan: _______________________________________

____

How I'll know I've achieved it: _______________________________

MY INTEREST / SKILL GOAL:

I want to: ____

By when: ____

My specific plan: _______________________________________

____

How I'll know I've achieved it: _______________________________

____

Accountability move: Tell one person about one of these goals. Write it somewhere you'll see it—a sticky note on your mirror, a phone wallpaper, the front of your planner. Out of sight, really, is out of mind with goals.

Bouncing Back—How to Handle Setbacks Without Giving Up

Here's the part nobody loves to talk about in goal-setting chapters: You are going to fail sometimes. Not sometimes—often. That's not pessimism. That's just what it means to be a person trying things, especially hard things.

The question isn't whether you'll have setbacks. It's what you do with them.

The Setback Response Framework

When something goes wrong—a goal gets derailed, a test goes badly, something you tried didn't work—here's the framework for responding in a way that keeps you moving forward:

1. **Feel it first.** Disappointment, frustration, embarrassment—these are real, and they deserve acknowledgment. You don't have to be relentlessly positive. "That was genuinely disappointing, and I'm allowed to feel that." Give yourself a time-limited window to feel it: an hour, an afternoon, a day. But set a limit.

2. **Get curious, not judgmental.** Instead of "I'm such a failure," ask: "What actually happened here?" Specifically. What went wrong? Was it preparation, execution, circumstances outside your control, or a goal that needed adjusting?

3. **Extract the lesson.** Every setback contains information. "Next time I'll…" Finish that sentence. Specifically.

4. **Adjust the plan, not the goal.** If you didn't reach a goal, the answer is usually not to abandon the goal—it's to change the strategy. What will you do differently this time?

5. **Take one step forward.** Any step. Small is fine. Taking a small action interrupts the pattern of staying stuck in the setback.

The "What Would I Tell a Friend?" Reset

When you're in the middle of a setback spiral, you've already met this technique in Chapter 8 for self-talk—and it applies here too. Imagine your best friend just went through the exact same setback. What would you say to them?

"You studied really hard, and it still didn't go the way you wanted. That's genuinely disappointing. But this one grade doesn't define your intelligence or your future. What can you do differently before the next test?"

Now say that to yourself. Word for word if you need to.

Understanding the Dip

Almost every meaningful skill or goal follows a pattern that looks like this:

Early progress → visible improvement → "The Dip" (plateau or apparent regression) → breakthrough → new level

The Dip is the part between early progress and breakthrough. It's where most people give up. It feels like proof that you're not getting better—but it's actually a sign that you're on the edge of a real leap. The practice is happening under the surface, even when the results aren't visible yet.

Understanding the Dip doesn't make it less frustrating. But it changes what it means. Instead of "I'm not improving, I should quit," it becomes: "I'm in the Dip. This is the part where I keep going."

> "I played guitar for eight months and felt like I was getting worse, not better. I almost quit. My teacher said I was hitting a plateau that happens to everyone and that I was actually closer to a breakthrough than I thought. Three weeks later, something clicked, and I could suddenly play things I hadn't been able to before. I'm so glad I didn't stop."
>
> — Lena, 7th grade

When to Adjust a Goal vs. When to Abandon It

Not every goal is worth pursuing forever. Here's how to tell the difference:

Adjust the goal when:

• The goal still matters to you but the timeline or strategy isn't working

• Circumstances changed and the original plan needs updating

• You've learned something new that makes a different approach smarter

• The goal was set too high too fast and needs to be broken into smaller steps

It's okay to release a goal when:

• You genuinely no longer care about it and never really did—it was someone else's goal for you

• Pursuing it is consistently making you miserable with no signs of meaningful progress

• It conflicts with something more important that you've discovered about yourself

• It was based on who you thought you should be, not who you actually are or want to become

Releasing a goal that no longer fits is not failure. It's self-knowledge. The skill is being honest with yourself about where you're at.

Celebrating Small Wins (Without Waiting for the Big Ones)

Here's a mistake almost everyone makes with goals: they set a big goal, work toward it, and plan to feel good about themselves when they achieve it. The finish line is where the celebration happens. The problem is that big goals take a long time. And if you only celebrate at the finish line, you spend most of the journey in a state of "not there yet" that quietly erodes motivation. Small wins change this. Not because you're lowering the bar—but because you're acknowledging the actual progress that's happening all along the way. And acknowledged progress compounds.

What Counts as a Win

A win doesn't have to be impressive to anyone else. It just has to be real. Here's what counts:

- You did the hard thing you've been avoiding for two weeks
- You showed up on a day when you really didn't want to
- You got a slightly better score than last time
- You asked for help instead of staying stuck
- You used a coping tool when you felt anxious instead of spiraling
- You said something true even though it was uncomfortable
- You tried something new and it didn't go great, but you tried
- You kept a good habit going for three days in a row
- You didn't give up on a hard problem
- You treated someone with kindness when you were in a bad mood

None of those make headlines. All of them move you forward.

How to Actually Celebrate (Beyond "Good Job" to Yourself)

Acknowledging a win properly—in a way your brain registers as meaningful—takes more than a passing thought. Here are ways to make small wins stick:

- **Write it down.** In your Glow Up Journal or Tracker. The act of writing it makes it more real and gives you a record to look back on.
- **Tell someone.** Not to brag—to share. "Hey, I finally did that thing I'd been putting off." The reaction of someone who cares about you —even a simple "That's great!"—reinforces the win neurologically.
- **Give yourself a specific reward.** Something small that you enjoy— an episode of a show, a treat you like, 20 minutes of gaming guilt-

free. The reward has to be intentionally connected to the win: "Because I did X, I get Y."

- **The physical anchor.** A fist pump, a quiet "Yes," a happy dance in your room. Your body participating in the celebration sends a signal to your brain that this moment matters.
- **Add it to your streak.** Track consecutive days of a habit in a calendar or app. The visual streak becomes its own motivation—you don't want to break it

.Glow Up Tracker Prompt: At the end of every week, write down one win —no matter how small. Over the course of a school year, that's forty wins. Forty moments of progress you would have forgotten if you hadn't written them down.

The Glow Up Yearbook—Documenting Your Middle School Journey

This is the culminating activity of the entire book. And it's one of the most meaningful things you can do at the end of a school year, a tough semester, or any significant chunk of your middle school experience.

The Glow Up Yearbook is not a formal document. It's not graded or evaluated. It's a record—in your own words—of who you were, what you went through, what you learned, and how you grew. It's for your eyes only, unless you choose otherwise. And when you look back at it in a year, or in five, you will be genuinely surprised by how much ground you've covered.

How to Build Your Glow Up Yearbook

You can do this in a dedicated notebook, in a digital document, in a notes app, or even as a private folder of voice memos. The format doesn't matter. The reflection does. Here are the prompts:

SECTION 1: WHERE I STARTED

This time last year (or when I started middle school), I was:

____

____

The thing I was most worried about:

____

The thing I thought I could never do:

____

The version of myself I was performing (vs. who I actually was):

____

____

SECTION 2: WHAT I WENT THROUGH

The hardest moment of this period:

____

____

The most embarrassing moment I survived:

____

A time I was really scared and did the thing anyway:

____

____

A friendship or relationship that taught me something:

____

____

Something that felt unfair that I had to deal with:

____

SECTION 3: WHAT I LEARNED

The most useful thing I learned about myself:

____

____

A skill I developed that I didn't have before:

____

Something I used to believe that I no longer believe:

____

____

A person who helped me grow (teacher, friend, family member, anyone):

____

What they taught me:

____

THE BEST ADVICE I received this year:

____

SECTION 4: HOW I GREW

Something I can do now that I couldn't do a year ago:

____

A way I handle hard things differently than I used to:

____

____

The proudest moment of this period — something I gave myself credit for:

____

____

One thing I like about who I'm becoming:

____

____

SECTION 5: WHERE I'M GOING

The version of myself I'm building toward:

____

____

One goal I'm carrying into the next chapter of my life:

____

____

Something I want to remember about this time, even the hard parts:

____

____

A message to my future self, one year from now:

____

____

____

____

The Glow Up Yearbook Ritual

Set aside an hour at the end of the school year — or at the end of each semester — to fill this out. Not rushed. Not distracted. Just you, your journal, and honest reflection.

Then seal it. Literally or metaphorically. Don't re-read it right away. Let it sit for at least three months. When you come back to it, you'll see yourself with new eyes. The gap between who you were when you wrote it and who you are when you read it is your growth, made visible.

> "I filled out something like this at the end of sixth grade and found it at the end of eighth grade. I didn't recognize the person who wrote it. Not in a bad way — just in a wow, I've come a long way kind of way. I cried a little. It was actually amazing to see."
>
> — Morgan, 9th grade

Growth Mindset and Goals Glow Up Tracker

Growth doesn't announce itself. It accumulates quietly in daily decisions — a fixed thought you caught and flipped, a goal you took one step toward, a setback you got back up from. This tracker helps you see that accumulation.

Week of:

____

FIXED MINDSET CATCH:

A fixed mindset thought I caught this week:

____

How I flipped it:

____

GOAL PROGRESS:

Goal I worked on this week:

____

Step I took:

____

Progress: ☐ Moving forward ☐ Stuck in the Dip ☐ Needs adjusting ☐ Achieved!

SETBACK CHECK:

Did I experience a setback this week? ☐ Yes ☐ No

If yes, how did I respond?

____

What did I learn from it?

____

WIN OF THE WEEK:

One small win I'm giving myself credit for (no win too small):

____

____

THE "YET" STATEMENT:

Something I'm not good at yet—and the one next step toward getting there:

____

____

GROWTH CONFIDENCE CHECK:

How much do I believe I can get better at hard things this week?

1 ---- 2 ---- 3 ---- 4 ---- 5 ---- 6 ---- 7 ---- 8 ---- 9 ---- 10

End-of-Semester Glow Up Review

• Which goal did I make the most progress on this semester?

• What was my biggest setback—and what did I actually do with it?

• What's one fixed mindset belief I started to loosen this semester?

• What's the win I'm most proud of that nobody else would know about?

• What do I want to be different—in my goals, my habits, or my mindset—
next semester?

• Is it time to fill out my Glow Up Yearbook? ☐ Yes—let's go.

You're Already Doing It

Here's what you now have in your final chapter toolkit:

• The fixed vs. growth mindset framework and how to catch and flip fixed
thoughts in real time

• The power of "yet"—two letters that keep every door open

• How to set SMART goals that are specific enough to actually act on

- Three categories of goals worth setting in middle school

- The Setback Response Framework—feel it, get curious, extract the lesson, adjust the plan, take one step

- The Dip—understanding why progress gets harder before it gets easier, and why that's actually a good sign

- How to celebrate small wins in ways your brain actually registers

- The Glow Up Yearbook—a full reflection system for documenting your growth across every dimension of middle school

You started this book looking for help surviving middle school. But the tools in this chapter—growth mindset, goal-setting, bouncing back, and celebrating progress—aren't just survival tools. They're the tools you'll use for the rest of your life to keep becoming whoever you're becoming.

And here's the thing about that: it never stops. The growth doesn't end when you graduate middle school, or high school, or any other milestone. You are always somewhere on the path. Always somewhere between who you were and who you're becoming.

The people who thrive in life are not the ones who never struggle. They're the ones who know how to keep going.

You're already one of those people. Time to turn the page.

final thoughts

YOU'VE GOT THIS — FOR REAL

You made it to the end of the book. That matters.

Not because finishing a book is some grand achievement, but because it means something about you: You took your own development seriously enough to show up, chapter after chapter, for yourself. In a world that's constantly pulling your attention in seventeen directions, that's actually hard to do.

So, what did we cover?

Everything You Now Know How to Do

• **Navigate the chaos of middle school's first days** (Chapter 1) — lockers, schedules, the social landscape, and decoding the unwritten rules

• **Make real friends, repair broken ones, and know when to walk away** (Chapter 2) — without losing yourself in the process

• **Drama-proof your social life** (Chapter 3) — gossip, rumors, group chat survival, toxic exits, and rebuilding trust after things fall apart

• **Protect yourself from bullying — and stand up for others** (Chapter 4) — verbally, socially, digitally, and when adults aren't helping

• **Stay organized when life is chaotic** (Chapter 5) — color systems, homework survival, test strategies, and the email that actually gets a response

• **Recover from awkward moments with your dignity intact** (Chapter 6) — the Three-Second Rule, presentation power moves, the Glow Up Journal

• **Manage stress, anxiety, and mood swings** (Chapter 7) — mindfulness hacks, panic plans, knowing when to ask for help

• **Like yourself — IRL and online** (Chapter 8) — the comparison trap, body changes, self-talk rewrites, the No Cap affirmation

• **Own your digital life** (Chapter 9) — what to post, how to protect your privacy, spotting red flags, building a reputation you're proud of

• **Communicate with everyone who matters** (Chapter 10) — teachers, parents, peers — with scripts for every situation, including the ones nobody teaches you

• **Take care of your body and brain** (Chapter 11) — sleep, food, movement, and intentional screen time as the foundation for everything else

• **Build the version of yourself you actually want to become** (Chapter 12) — growth mindset, real goal setting, bouncing back, celebrating small wins, and the Glow Up Yearbook

One Last Honest Thing

Middle school is hard. Not "just push through it" hard — genuinely, legitimately hard. Your brain is under construction. Your body is changing. Your social world is more complicated than it's ever been. You're figuring out who you are while surrounded by hundreds of other people who are also trying to figure out who they are. That's a lot.

The tools in this book don't make it easy. Nothing makes it easy. But they make it more navigable. They give you something to reach for when you're in the middle of a hard moment, and your brain goes blank. They give you language for things that used to just feel like confusion.

You are not going to use every tool in this book perfectly. You're going to forget some of them. You're going to have bad days where nothing works, and you just need to sleep and try again tomorrow. That is completely fine. That is, in fact, the whole point.

Growth isn't a straight line. It looks more like this: two steps forward, one back, sideways for a little while, a sudden leap, a confusing plateau, then forward again. If you're paying attention, even the sideways parts teach you something.

The only thing that actually matters: Keep going. Keep trying. Keep being curious about who you're becoming. That's the whole game.

Carry This With You

When things get hard — and they will — come back to the parts that help. The book doesn't have to be read in order. It doesn't have to be read all at once.

Flip to the chapter that matches whatever you're dealing with right now. Use the scripts when you need words. Fill in the trackers to see your own progress. Write in the Glow Up Journal when you need to get out of your head.

This is a reference, not a one-time read. The middle of a hard friendship situation is exactly when to flip to Chapter 2. The night before a presentation you're dreading is exactly when Chapter 6 earns its spot on your shelf.

Final Words

You are a person in progress. Not a finished product. Not someone who needs to have it all figured out. A person who is actively becoming—making mistakes and learning from them, trying hard things and surviving them, showing up for yourself and for the people you care about, even when it's uncomfortable.

That's not a middle school thing. That's a you thing. And you've clearly got it.

Now go handle it.

www.ingramcontent.com/pod-product-compliance
Lightning Source LLC
Chambersburg PA
CBHW051412050726
47595CB00010B/4032